ON EDGE

International Banking and Country Risk

Ellen S. Goldberg
Dan Haendel

PRAEGER

New York
Westport, Connecticut
London

To our daughters,
Tamar and Rebecca

Library of Congress Cataloging-in-Publication Data

Goldberg, Ellen S.
  On edge.

  Bibliography: p.
  Includes index.
  1. Banks and banking, International.   2. Country
risk.   I. Haendel, Dan, 1950-   . II. Title.
HG3881.G6142 1987   332.1'5   86-25324
ISBN 0-275-92604-4 (alk. paper)

Library of Congress Catalog Card Number: 86-25324
ISBN: 0-275-92604-4

First published in 1987

Praeger Publishers, 521 Fifth Avenue, New York, NY 10175
A division of Greenwood Press, Inc.

Printed in the United States of America

∞
The paper used in this book complies with the
Permanent Paper Standard issued by the National
Information Standards Organization (Z39.48-1984).

10 9 8 7 6 5 4 3 2 1

332.15
G6180
235027

Contents

Foreword

Since August 1982 when Mexico announced that it had run out of foreign exchange, the debt crisis has made front page news. The debt bomb is still ticking, threatening the international financial system. Import reductions in cash-strapped developing countries have meant losses of exports and thus jobs in the United States. The economic problems pale, however, compared to the political one: social and political upheaval in debt burdened countries is fertile ground for insurgency. Peru is struggling with a Maoist movement, the Philippines with communist insurgencies and Mexico's ruling party is weakening. Ultimately, instability could result in a flood of refugees that would be impossible to stem. Because of these concerns, the debt issue is high on the agenda of 1988 U.S. presidential candidates.

On Edge by Ellen S. Goldberg and Dan Haendel should be read by everybody. It is an important and good account of the origin of the crisis and the current situation, and the interests of the parties concerned. The points of view of commercial bankers, debtors, regulators and governments are described in a balanced way. For the layman, the authors will help reconstruct the puzzle; for the academic, the book should serve well anybody interested in international affairs. Indeed, the book fills a vacuum which currently exists. *On Edge* gives a fair view of the problem we face and describes the various proposals that have been put forward to deal with the crisis.

The debt crisis is a long-term economic and political barrier to development that is slowly strangling world economic growth. One year after the Baker Plan was announced at the October 1985 annual meeting of the International Bank for Reconstruction and Development (World Bank) and the International Monetary Fund (IMF), creditors are more reluctant than ever to lend and debtors increasingly are wondering about the benefits of borrowing more. Latin Americans fear the backlash of prolonged recessions due to the strain of debt servicing. With interest payments alone consuming on average over 40 percent of exports, real per capita incomes have slipped back to their 1970 levels and the 1980s seem like a lost decade for development.

Although its magnitude is unprecedented, the debt crisis is not a new phenomenon. In the nineteenth century, nine state governments in the United States suspended their debt-service payments. Britain and France defaulted on payments to the United States during the 1930s ''on the grounds that their obligations to meet the needs of their people were greater than the legal obligations to creditors.'' As recently as 1953, the United States reduced Germany's debt by two-thirds and stretched the payment over 35 years at a concessional interest rate of only 3 percent.

In the United States most corporate restructurings and workouts under Bankruptcy Code (Chapter 11) involve reductions of debt outstanding as well as concessions on interest rates. New debts are used to restructure the corporation and give it breathing space. The presumption in corporate restructurings is that it is in everybody's interest to keep the corporation alive and that ultimately the value of creditor's claims will be enhanced by the restructuring. However, under the current strategy for developing countries the creditors insist that all debt be serviced at market interest rates on a timely basis. In fact, those debtors in the worst condition typically are paying the highest prices. Banks, pressured by the U.S. government and the IMF, have lent additional billions to big debtors such as Mexico. Typically, little if any new money has been made available to small debtors (those that do not individually threaten the international financial system) and these debtors have been charged higher interest rates. Despite some individual defiance, most prominently by Peru's President Alan Garcia, debtors have shied away from threats; a debtors cartel has not been formed, although over time debtors have increased their informal exchange of information. At the 1986 IBRD/IMF annual meeting, the chief negotiators for both Mexico's and Argentina's debt were sipping coffee together, bending over charts and numbers.

In the absence of the international equivalent of the Chapter 11 Bankruptcy Code, banks have required countries to continue making full payments of interest. No bank wants to be first to grant concessions; also, the U.S. government, through the Federal Reserve System, the U.S. Treasury, and the various regulatory agencies, has encouraged the banks to lend more money on the grounds that such lending will help debtor nations to grow out of their difficulties.

But this scenario works best if one assumes a favorable world economic environment, namely 3 percent or more in economic growth and a standstill on protectionist tendencies in industrial countries. For debt-service burdens to become more manageable, real dollar interest rates would have to be lower. Finally, banks would have to be prepared to provide new credits, increasing their exposure at an annual rate of 5 to 7 percent from now until the end of the decade. Governments too—through their export credit agencies and through bilateral assistance—should play a key role by providing loans at subsidized rates. But until now these favorable assumptions have not come true.

One private sector initiative, the secondary market for LDC debt, has made a small dent in the stock of debt. In this market, debt-for-equity swaps have for some countries reduced their indebtedness and replaced it by additional investments in the local economy. In the secondary market, typically multinational corporations have been buying up government foreign currency debts at a discount and then converting the funds back into local currency (at the Central Bank also at a discount) to finance new plants and/or equipment.

Without some debt alleviation, a number of countries are unlikely to ever get back on their feet. As long as their debt is growing faster than their net export proceeds, they will never catch up. For these countries, the bank and industrial governments should consider writing off part of the debt. There would not be any major consequences for banks or governments provided that countries benefiting from such a "radical" treatment do not present a risk to the international financial system. The difficulty of such an approach is to find criteria to determine where the borderline should be drawn. In fact, a number of banks have already written down, though they have not written off, a sizable portion of their exposure to small debtors. These countries still have a contractual obligation to pay interest on the total amount of debt outstanding. A write-off by the banks for some countries would obviously have to be reviewed carefully, to examine the possibility that the debtor could further reduce imports, adjust its economy, or generate additional exports. To avoid any abrupt reduction of bank earnings, U.S. regulators and Congress might have to allow an extended period for the banks actually to write off such loans. A clause to guard against free rides would have to be included. Such a clause would stipulate that in the event a country enjoys a sudden, unexpected increase in foreign exchange receipts, for example because of a jump in copper prices, debt cancellations would be reviewed.

Moreover, even for those countries that are better off, some way has to be devised to increase investments, because as Juan Vital Surrouille, Minister of Economy for Argentina said, "The decision to grow is not negotiable."[1] One way to combine debt servicing with faster growth would be to consider a formula which would establish a country's debt-service payments as a function of its export receipts and non-tied capital inflows. During the 1970s, a debt-service ratio of 20–25 percent was considered very high.

Today the debt-service ratios of many debtors are in the 40–50 percent range (even after rescheduling takes place). But the fact that such levels have become a sort of norm does not mean that they are sustainable. Under a flexible formula a country would allocate a portion of its foreign exchange receipts to debt service. The details of the formula and the exact percentages should be established on a case-by-case basis. The difference, if any, between the payments dictated by the formula and the interest actually due could be capitalized.

To stimulate growth, an additional portion of debtor countries' export receipts could be set aside in a trust fund either in local currency or in foreign exchange. The debtor government would use the money in this fund to make investments in productive sectors, to complete priority projects, and to inject capital into the private sector. In return for the reduction in debt-service payments, the debtor would allow a mechanism to be put in place to monitor the allocation of money in the trust fund, to ensure that it is invested appropriately.

---

1. Statement by the Honorable Juan Vital Surrouille, Minister of Economy and Governor of the IMF for Argentina on behalf of Latin American countries, Spain and the Philippines at the 1986 IBRD/IMF Annual Meeting, September 30, 1986, Washington, D.C.

The issue of third world debt is here to stay. It is further complicated by the emergence of the United States as a major debtor and the slide of other industrial countries—such as Australia—into the debt trap. Imbalances in the world have become greater: commodity prices are at a historical low—not only oil but also wheat and copper. Exchange rates are more volatile than ever, technology is advancing, globalization of financial and capital markets in industrial countries is happening; the world economy increasingly is managed by the ''haves'' while the ''have-nots'' are left behind. The challenge posed by the third world debt crisis is to devise ways to get these countries back on their feet. Too much is at stake. *On Edge* is the primer everybody should read to understand the dimension of today's debt threat.

CHRISTINE A. BOGDANOWICZ-BINDERT—

Senior Vice President
Shearson Lehman Brothers Inc.

Acknowledgments

Invitations to one of the authors to discuss the foreign debt crisis with business executives at the Brookings Institution and with government and military officials at the National War College prompted the preparation of this book. The authors further developed the initial ideas during seminars on international financial institutions and international banking offered at Georgetown University's School of Business Administration.

The authors gratefully acknowledge the assistance of numerous individuals who reviewed drafts of the manuscript and offered useful and necessary corrections and suggestions. Although several members of the financial community have preferred to remain anonymous, the authors wish to thank them, as well as the following individuals: Doug Kruse (formerly with the Department of the Treasury and currently with Merrill Lynch); Betty Whelchel (formerly with the Department of the Treasury and currently with Sherman and Sterling); Pamela Smith; Russell Munk—who reviewed the manuscript for the Treasury—of the Department of the Treasury; Michael Aho of the Council on Foreign Relations; John Yochelson of the Center for Strategic and International Studies; Michael Czinkota of the National Center for Export-Import Studies (NCEIS); and Christine A. Bogdanowicz-Bindert of Shearson Lehman Brothers Inc.

NCEIS, a nonprofit, nonpartisan organization, was established in 1981 at Georgetown University to encourage acceptable trade policies among nations and to improve the trade practices of firms. NCEIS assisted in arranging the publication of this book. The views expressed in this book are solely those of the authors and not necessarily those of the U.S. Department of the Treasury.

1

Introduction

In August 1982, Mexico's financial crisis focused attention on the plight of key debtor countries and the accompanying vulnerability of major international banks from their international lending operations. International banks had made loans to developing countries' governments and state-owned companies, as well as to private companies located there. The debt problems of several developing countries were already severe when Mexico suddenly announced its inability to service its debt. Brazil's debt difficulties surfaced shortly thereafter. The gravity of the situation was reflected in the debt-servicing obligations of major debtor countries. For example, the foreign debt payments of Mexico, Brazil, and Argentina had increased to well over 100 percent of their annual export receipts. The foreign debt burden of developing countries was then about $750 billion. Most of these countries also experienced massive capital flight as their residents lost confidence in the health of their economies. A sharp drop in their export earnings, caused by a stagnant world trading environment and a dramatic fall in their commodity prices, combined with rising real interest rates to squeeze their foreign debt-service capabilities. Several key debtor countries stood on the verge of financial collapse and threatened the viability of the international financial system.[1]

Following on the heels of Mexico's debt crisis, the International Monetary Fund (IMF)– World Bank 1982 meetings in Toronto were held in an ominous atmosphere. The international community responded by treating the debt crisis as a case of a short-term liquidity squeeze, not insolvency or chronic growth problems, and adopted an IMF-centered approach that included the adoption of IMF adjustment programs and the continuation of commercial bank lending. However, the near panic of 1982 gave way to a sense of relief, perhaps even complacency, as time passed. Some observers considered Argentina's 1984 agreement with its creditors as the end of the first phase of the debt crisis and most participants agreed that a potential disaster had been averted. Several key debtor countries began to adopt needed adjustment programs, and the outlines of an economic recovery started to appear. By 1985 real interest rates, although still relatively high at about 6 percent, had come down from their peak of nearly 10 percent. The U.S. economic recovery, even if not assured of durability, had begun to take hold. Increased economic activity in the industrial countries stimulated some growth in developing countries as demand for their commodities generated a price rebound.[2] Nevertheless, anxiety about the ultimate resolution of the debt crisis has spawned periodic feelings of panic and relief among international bankers, leaders of debtor countries, bank regulators, and other participants.

In 1982, fears of default by key debtors caused considerable anxiety throughout the international financial system. Since then, the potential risk emanating from the stringent adjustments these countries have had to undertake and their continued commitment to maintain them have eroded the confidence previously associated with international lending. Uncertainty characterizes numerous dimensions of the debt problem and has not served to inspire confidence regarding future developments. For example, the consequences of the domestic difficulties confronting the debtor countries remain unclear, many of them have fallen out of compliance with their IMF programs, and there appears to be a lack of consensus regarding the measures necessary to cope with, if not solve, the debt problem. A plan unveiled by U.S. Secretary of the Treasury James Baker at the October 1985 IMF–World Bank meeting in Seoul, Korea, has been criticized by the debtor countries and some policymakers as "too little too late" and lacking in implementation.[3]

Even the most optimistic projections of world trade growth reflect an awareness of the fragility of bringing key debtor countries' debt-servicing capabilities in line with their foreign debt burden. The rescheduling of these countries' debts, while ameliorating their present difficulties by postponing the problem and buying the key ingredient of time needed for debtor countries to adjust, in and of itself has not, thus far, been a solution. New loans to service prior debt have added to the already heavy burden and raise the question whether such additional loans are the appropriate remedy for the debt problem. On the basis of this evidence, some have concluded that some form of debt relief is necessary because there is no arithmetic solution to the debt problem.[4] Others are concerned that a future downturn in the business cycle could result in a greater burden for the debtors and suggest that a variety of contingency plans are needed. Advocates of debt relief proposals are often concerned about the political repercussions of austerity programs.[5] In addition to acknowledging the political dimension of the financial strains, they fear that the strains in debtor countries may create a "political pressure cooker" and lead to political and social upheavals.[6] Since the debt problem is concentrated in Latin America, the United States has also been cognizant of the national security dimension of the issue.

Chronic threats to the viability of the international banking and financial system have stimulated reactions by debtor countries, commercial banks, regulators, and international institutions. These harrowing financial encounters have taken on the flavor of a perpetual "Perils of Pauline" saga. There are moments of terror—as the heroine is tied to the railroad tracks and the fast-moving train approaches—followed by relief when the rescue occurs. Whether the ad hoc rescue packages placed in operation primarily during the 1982–1984 period will ensure a happy ending remains to be seen.

ROOTS OF THE PROBLEM

Experts disagree over the degree of importance ascribed to the factors causing the global debt problem. Nonetheless, there appears to be general agreement that, although debtor countries faced unique conditions and made a number of errors in their domestic financial policies and activities, several causes were outside their immediate control: the 1974 oil price hike, alternating periods of global inflation and recession during the 1970s, the second oil shock in 1979, high "real" interest rates by the early 1980s, falling commodity prices, and a "strong" dollar.

The severity of the international financial difficulties currently confronting the world community is often traced to the 1974 fourfold oil-price increases imposed by OPEC (Organization of Petroleum Exporting Countries). That event fueled persistent inflation and stimulated cyclical economic fluctuations that included periods of global recession. The effects on the balance of payments position of many countries were dramatic. As developing countries looked to the commercial banks for loans, chronic expansion and contraction of the international economic system made the task of private international bankers increasingly difficult.

The international banking and financial system sought to grapple with the 1974 oil shock through the process of *petrodollar recycling*. Oil exporters such as Kuwait and Saudi Arabia looked for safe havens to invest the surplus capital generated by their growing oil revenues. Given their initial aversion to risk, many of the Arab oil exporters invested their surplus oil earnings in money-center U.S. banks, such as Citibank, Chase Manhattan, Bank of America, and Manufacturers Hanover, as well as numerous key Western European and Japanese banks.

These international banks, in turn, increased their loans to developing countries, especially those with relatively higher incomes and considered to have well-managed economies. This was the genesis of loan concentration in Latin American countries. International banks were motivated to undertake these loans because of the higher earnings they were initially able to generate and satisfied themselves that the risk associated with such loans was relatively low. Developing countries sought these loans from private banks, which were becoming their primary source of external capital. Ironically, this massive capital transfer over-shadowed demands enshrined in calls for a New International Economic Order. Official creditors were unable to meet the financing demands of developing countries for their development plans and commercial banks did not impose the conditionality requirements, that is, the agreement by the debtor to undertake certain adjustment policies in order to obtain credit, of the international financial institutions. By the end of 1975, loans from the world's private international banks to developing countries stood at approximately $70 billion, a sum already considered of significance at that time.[7]

Critics of the way "petrodollar recycling" was unfolding argued that the international banks were lowering their lending standards by making such large loans to these developing countries. Perhaps even more significant was the criticism that these loans were being concentrated in a limited number of developing countries, by a limited number of major banks. Serious questions were also raised about the banks' capital adequacy and reserves to meet potential losses or delays in repayment, especially as the debt service ratios of such countries climbed dramatically. However, the initial concerns expressed by these critics regarding the process of international lending to developing countries were either ignored or dismissed as alarmist.

This initial concentration was a precursor to the precarious profile and exposure the international banks would generate by the early 1980s. Furthermore, as early as 1977, concerns were being raised about major commercial banks' loss of freedom of action on grounds they could not risk the consequences of a significant decline in lending to major debtor countries. In short, the massive amounts of such bank loans would act as a telling constraint on the formulation of their strategies to shake off the yoke of Third World loans.

Triggered by the turmoil accompanying the shah of Iran's fall, the 1979 oil price increases forced the international financial system to adjust to another shock. The recession of 1974–1975 was followed by the high inflation rate of the late 1970s. Rather than continuing with inflationary policies, however, the U.S. government led the way in combating high inflation rampant in the U.S. and international economic system by adopting restrictive monetary policies, resulting in high "real" interest rates followed by a relatively "strong" dollar. These measures contributed to a global recession in the early 1980s that exacerbated the debt burden already afflicting key developing countries.[8]

The combination of these factors made debtor countries' floating-rate loans, usually denominated in dollars, an increasingly onerous burden to service. Many key developing countries found themselves unable to service their foreign debts. To maintain their creditworthiness, several countries concluded they had little choice but to agree to adopt politically unpopular IMF adjustment programs that include cutting domestic spending and growth, for example.

Oil-exporting countries were not exempt from the effects of the global recession. Countries such as Saudi Arabia, Nigeria, Mexico, and Venezuela had launched massive development programs during the 1970s, and several borrowed heavily to finance them. The 1981–1982 drop in the price of oil and reduction in global demand created some economic and social difficulties for a number of oil-exporting countries, especially those with large populations to support. Despite the financing problems of several of these countries, their problems pale in comparison with those of developing countries that rely on limited commodity exports.

BANK LENDING AND THE DEBT BURDEN

The focus of this work is on the vulnerability of the international banks, especially U.S. banks, and their relationship with their leading country debtors. Increasingly concerned about the threats posed by their foreign lending exposure to a few key debtors, the potentially negative impact on earnings, and adverse publicity, international commercial banks have been profoundly challenged by the debt problem.[9] Major U.S. banks and bank regulators may well have preferred to reduce the concentration of loans to key developing countries immediately, but an orderly resolution of the debt problem precluded such measures.

Most major international banks had done a considerable amount of country risk analysis but, due in part to inadequate information, were nonetheless surprised by the sheer size and concentration of the debt leading debtors had accumulated and the difficulties they subsequently encountered servicing these debts. Concern about the ability and willingness of debtor countries to service their loans, the crux of country risk, disturbed an element at the very core of banking—confidence.

The nervous response of the private banking community to the recognition of the seriousness of the debt problems confronting key developing countries was reflected in their initial efforts to "cut and run" and thereby curtail their significant exposure. Although the withdrawal of many smaller banks with sufficiently low exposure placed even greater pressure on the money-center international banks, the major banks were fully aware of the severe constraint exerted by their objective of maintaining the value of their outstanding loans. If the major banks had cut back their lending more sharply than they did, such that debtor countries could not service their outstanding loans, those loans would be of doubtful value, and the viability of the lender would be severely eroded.

To forestall the possibility of such a commercial bank withdrawal, provide key debtors with liquidity, and maintain the integrity of the international financial and banking system, international financial institutions, especially the IMF and BIS (Bank for International Settlements), and leading industrialized countries took the initiative and helped maintain confidence.[10] These parties extended a number of bridge financing arrangements and prepared what has been labeled "package funding," that is, a financing arrangement for additional capital that includes the participation of the IMF, the BIS, and a number of industrialized countries. This package then served as the basis, indeed a condition, for what has been called "coercive" or "involuntary lending." Former U.S. Secretary of Treasury Regan has explained it as a process of "bailing in" the commercial banks. By extending additional loans to leading debtor countries, rather than cutting such countries off from new loans as had been done in previous reschedulings, major banks increased their exposure to such countries as Mexico, Brazil, and Argentina, even if at a slower rate than in the past.

Loan reschedulings for both private and official debts have become commonplace, as debtor countries could not meet their debt-servicing payments. The terms of the initial reschedulings often led to an ironic result for both the debtor and creditor. The reason such a debtor country reschedules its debt lies in its very inability to service it, yet a higher interest rate and renegotiation fees to compensate for the increased risk will require even larger future payments. Accordingly, the focus of recent rescheduling negotiations has been on improving the terms and making payments more manageable, especially as the total amount of developing country debt continues to escalate, having reached nearly $1 trillion by 1986.

Most debtor countries have been careful to cooperate and adopt measures necessary to maintain their debt-servicing obligations, in large part, to maintain their access to the international capital markets. Perhaps mindful of the consequences for Mexico after its default at the beginning of the twentieth century when it was unable to raise capital in the world markets for about 50 years, debtor countries have been careful to avoid bringing matters to a flash point.[11] Despite occasional debtor cartel scares and talk of debt moratoriums, debtor countries, in most cases, have opted instead to channel their energies into renegotiating the terms of their debt obligations. In short, the debt problem has created a certain convergence of interests among creditors and debtors to resolve the issue satisfactorily. However, tension exists regarding the appropriate allocation of the burden to be borne by each of the parties and persistent threats of default or other forms of unilateral actions, such as limiting debt servicing to a percentage of export earnings, have had an unsettling effect on the international financial market. Indeed, there have been efforts, such as Fidel Castro's mid-1985 debt conference, to seize the initiative and gain political advantage from the debt crisis.

Some critics argue that the "state of crisis" in international lending "has been managed by an ad hoc policy of 'muddle through' in a gamble for time," that is, time for the world economy to recover "quickly and strongly enough to restore confidence in the debt-service ability of the major borrowing countries."[12] With debt service payments by developing countries exceeding new borrowings by approximately $25 billion in 1985, a vicious cycle exacerbated by low commodity prices and a slowdown in trade has prevented debtor countries from being able to obtain sufficient lending to generate the economic growth necessary to service their debts and restore their creditworthiness.[13] Addressing these worrisome developments, the Baker Plan reflects increased U.S. concern regarding the welfare of the U.S. banking system and debtor countries. The U.S. government's involvement in the search for a viable framework for a solution has sought to preempt the adoption of radical proposals by major debtor countries. Furthermore, the United States has signaled that it no longer views the debt problem as a temporary and isolated liquidity squeeze, but rather sees it as a long-term and chronic economic and financial problem. To secure the cooperation of the parties, the U.S. government drew the conclusion that austerity as a solution for the debt crisis should be replaced by a strategy of growth.[14]

The shifting roles of the participants in the unfolding debt drama have been superimposed on the varying perspectives and interests of the parties. Although the relationship between international bankers and debtor countries is essential and may, indeed, constitute the primary dealings in debt negotiations, it provides only a partial view of the complex web of interactions that place constraints in the unfolding drama. Equally critical is an understanding of the motives, interests, objectives, and strategies, which although conflicting are often assumed to be identical, of other parties—creditor governments, bank regulatory agencies, the IMF, the World Bank, and even the BIS.

We will focus on the implications of the global debt problem for international banks by examining the issue from the perspective of each of the leading players. Starting with the policies, objectives, and actions of debtor governments, we proceed to analyze the assumptions, behavior, and strategies of international banks and their regulators, as well as the role of such institutions as the IMF. In addition, we will examine the course of action creditors chose to cope with the crisis as well as a number of suggested alternative solutions to resolve the global debt problem. We will examine the pressures on bank regulators to improve the "rules of the game" in international lending as a way of ensuring that the future does not yield even more ominous global debt problems.

NOTES

1. R.T. McNamar, "The International Debt Problem: Working Out a Solution," Philadelphia, Pennsylvania: Fifth International Monetary and Trade Conference, December 5, 1983.

2. *The Banker*, "Making It Fit," September 1983, p. 5.

3. Intergovernmental Group of Twenty-Four on International Monetary Affairs, Buenos Aires Communiqué, March 6, 1986; Charles E. Schumer, "Ease Up on Debtor Nations, New York *Times*, March 10, 1986.

4. Alfred J. Watkins, *Till Debt Do Us Part* (Washington, D.C.: Roosevelt Center for American Policy Studies, 1986).

5. Henry A. Kissinger, "Those Latin Debts," The Washington *Post*, June 24, 1984.

6. Lawrence Rout, "Future Political Effect of Foreign-Debt Crisis Worry Some Bankers," *The Wall Street Journal*, June 30, 1983.

7. See G.A. Costanzo (vice chairman, Citicorp) and Irving S. Friedman, *The Emerging Role of Private Banks in the Developing World* (New York: Citicorp, 1977), p. 1.

8. *Economic Report of the President* (Washington, D.C.: United States Government Printing Office, 1984), ch. 2.

9. Jack M. Guttentag and Richard J. Herring, *The Current Crisis in International Lending* (Washington, D.C.: The Brookings Institution, 1985).

10. *The World Bank Annual Report,* 1983, p. 31.

11. Andre Gunder Frank, "Can the Debt Bomb Be Defused?" *World Policy Journal,* Summer 1984.

12. Guttentag and Herring, op. cit., p. 1.

13. *Development and Debt Service: Dilemma of 1980s—Abridged 1985–86 World Debt Tables* (Washington, D.C.: The World Bank, March 27, 1986).

14. Christine A. Bogdanowicz-Bindert, "World Debt: The United States Reconsiders," *Foreign Affairs,* Winter 1985–1986.

2

The Plight of the Debtor Countries

A variety of views exists with respect to the analysis of the debt crisis, the implications to be drawn from it, and the steps needed for its successful resolution. Some contend that the debt problem is global and systemic in nature. Others argue that it is better understood and operationally managed as a series of unique country adjustment situations. Yet another perspective considers it in essence a regional Latin American crisis.[1] The plight of key debtor countries has been attributed to their ''overborrowing'' to finance budget deficits and development projects, although it has also been cast in terms of nonprudent ''overlending'' by international commercial banks. In either case, the impact on the debtors and their creditors has been dramatic as they have struggled to cope with a situation of unknown consequences, with worrisome prospects for the participants.

A PROFILE OF THE DEBTOR COUNTRIES

The bulk of commercial bank lending to developing countries is outstanding to a relatively small number of states, particularly those of Latin America, as shown in Table 2.1. Newly industrialized countries in Latin America were especially adroit in generating their growth by increasing their borrowing. Their thirst for funds coincided with the interests of international banks whose petrodollar recycling involved lending funds to such borrowers. During the 1970s, Mexico and Brazil were consuming more than one-half of the total new financial loans commercial banks extended to developing countries. Combined with Chile, Argentina, and South Korea, these countries also financed a substantial amount of their current account deficit by increasing their bank borrowing.

Although there is an understandable temptation to lump all developing countries into one category, a differentiation of their strengths and vulnerabilities may provide greater understanding of their ability to cope with their foreign debt problems. Developing countries can be differentiated on the basis of various criteria.

- The Newly Industrialized Countries (NICs)—Brazil is usually advanced as the best example—have premised their prospects on substantial growth based on investments in manufacturing, industrial projects, and similar means of rapid development. A number of middle-income countries, some with large populations, have looked to foreign lending to maintain their growth and standard of living. Many Latin American countries have in the past relied on commercial loans for such purposes, while most East Asian countries have avoided the most severe aspects of the debt problem.

- OPEC and other oil producing countries have sought to transform their economies by major, sometimes grandiose, development programs. Yet these oil producers may also be distinguished by those that have large populations to support and those that do not. The decline in oil prices during the 1980s has had a significant negative impact on such oil-exporting countries as Mexico, Nigeria, and Venezuela.

- Low-income countries, sometimes referred to as the Fourth World, are so devoid of natural or human resources that they have little opportunity to merit creditworthiness from commercial banks and usually seek bilateral foreign aid or multilateral concessional assistance to survive. Many African countries are in this category and have had severe difficulties in servicing their obligations to the multilateral financial institutions that serve as their creditors.

Quite naturally, the newly industrialized and the oil-producing countries have been the most significant private and public borrowers. The newly industrialized countries of Latin America (such as Brazil and Mexico), and East Asia (for example, Taiwan, South Korea, Hong Kong, and Singapore) proved most successful in diversifying their economic base and stimulating economic growth as well as exports.[2] The relative success of most East Asian countries in avoiding the harsher dimensions of the debt crisis confronting many Latin American countries has been attributed to their flexible economies, relatively free exchange rate policies, and absence of major subsidies or price distortions.[3]

Some oil-exporting countries, on the other hand, are almost totally dependent on this one commodity for their foreign exchange receipts. For example, in 1979 oil provided Venezuela and Algeria with 98 percent of their income, Iran with 95 percent, Nigeria with 91 percent, and Indonesia with 69 percent. Those countries with large populations to support felt the pressure of the oil price drop most acutely.[4]

In many cases, developing countries accumulated large debts, often to maintain domestic activity to finance consumption, rather than stimulate future economic growth.

TABLE 2.1. The World's Leading Debtors, 1983 (in billions of dollars)

	Total (end of 1983)	Loans from Private Banks	Unguaranteed Bank Debt	Payment as % of Annual Export Earnings (includes short-term obligations)
Brazil	93	67	55	117
Mexico	90	68	61	146
Argentina	45	27	22	230
South Korea	40	21	—	65
Venezuela	38	29	22	107
Indonesia	30	10	—	35
Israel	30	—	—	156
Poland	27	24	10	85
Philippines	26	14	8	173
Turkey	24	12	10	82
USSR	23	—	—	50
Egypt	19	—	—	80
Yugoslavia	19	11	8	45
Chile	18	12	10	140
Nigeria	17	12	6	57
Algeria	15	—	—	41
East Germany	14	—	—	83
Peru	12	6	4	110
Columbia	10	6	—	118
Rumania	10	—	—	61
Thailand	10	8	—	50

Sources: Art Pine, "International Bankers Take Steps to Restore Faith in Their System," *The Wall Street Journal*, September 15, 1982. *Time*, "The Debt-Bomb Threat," January 10, 1983, p. 43. Michael Edgerton, "Western Banks, Poor Nations Co-Star in Drama of Global Debt," *Chicago Tribune*, June 10, 1983. *The Wall Street Journal*, "World Debt in Crisis," June 22, 1984, pp. 35-39. Federal Reserve Bank of New York, "Economic Dimensions of LDC Debt," May 1984. The AMEX Bank Review, *International Bank Debt and the LDCs*, London: American Express International Banking Corporation, 1984. *Debt and the Developing Countries*, Washington, D.C.: The World Bank, 1984. *The American Banker*, "International Briefing," August 8, 1984.

The principal policy failures were in the use of commercial bank loans to maintain consumption rather than to increase investment, the subsidization of agricultural goods consumption rather than the adoption of appropriate incentives to encourage agricultural production and the maintenance of excessively high exchange rates. Moreover, in many countries, little effort was made to reduce severe inequities in income distribution.[5]

Other assessments are even less charitable. "Resources have been wasted, economic mismanagement—and corruption in some cases—have taken their toll."[6]

As key debtor countries confronted their debt-servicing difficulties, it was not clear initially whether these were unique and isolated cases that could be managed on an ad hoc or case-by-case basis. Even though international banks and institutions had been able to cope with the debt problems experienced during the late 1970s and early 1980s by countries such as Zaire, Sudan, Peru, and Turkey, the size and scope of the debt burden of key developing countries raised a serious question whether the international financial system was facing a threat of a different order of magnitude. "Financial institutions and government leaders had not dealt with problems of this magnitude and number. No one fully understood the nature or dimensions of the problem. Yet, through the leadership of the U.S. monetary authorities, the IMF, the BIS, and the cooperation of commercial banks and other creditor governments, disaster was avoided."[7]

Mexico's sudden admission of its inability to service its debt obligations was the first sign of the significant difference presented by this debt crisis, in particular, the threat it posed. The individual and collective financial squeeze of the leading debtor countries was considered to pose a significant threat to the viability of the international financial system. The United States made an initial decision to manage the crisis on a case-by-case basis on the assumption that the problem was one of illiquidity, not insolvency. Furthermore, the approach for coping with the problems of these debtors would establish a pattern and framework for dealing with the others that were to follow. An examination of the plight and adjustments of several of the leading debtor countries provides useful insights into the differences and similarities in dealing with their debt-servicing obligations.

Mexico

Mexico's severe liquidity crunch of August 1982, when it ran out of foreign exchange to service its approximately $80 billion foreign debt, directed the attention of the international financial community to what *Time* magazine labeled the impending debt bomb.[8] "The debt problem is usually dated as beginning on Thursday, August 12, 1982. On that day, Mexico's recently appointed Finance Minister, Jesus Silva-Herzog, called the Treasury to say that Mexico would completely exhaust its foreign exchange reserve by the following Monday."[9]

Mexico's liquidity squeeze stemmed from a simultaneous combination of factors. Its falling oil revenues coincided with high floating interest rates on its loans. Mexico's policy of maintaining an overvalued peso spurred private capital outflows and depleted its foreign exchange reserves, which Mexico initially sought to finance through loans of shorter maturities.[10] During an intensive weekend in mid-August 1982, a multifaceted financial package was put in place for Mexico.[11] A key part of the Mexican financing package was not only the bridging to an IMF program and drawings, but also U.S. government agreement to provide Mexico with $1 billion in Commodity Credit Corporation guarantees as well as an advance $1 billion payment by the U.S. Strategic Petroleum Reserve for oil.[12] This was an innovative way for the United States to achieve the dual purposes of providing needed liquidity for Mexico while acquiring oil at a reasonable price.

The U.S. Department of the Treasury's Exchange Stabilization Fund (ESF) entered into a $600 million swap arrangement in the form of Mexican peso/U.S. dollar swaps with the Bank of Mexico, simultaneous with a $325 million swap entered into by the Federal Reserve System. These arrangements were parallel to a $925 million credit arrangement between the Bank of Mexico and the Bank for International Settlements (BIS). The BIS has played a critical role in several ad hoc financing arrangements by providing short-term loans to key debtor countries as a bridge to the longer-term restructuring of commercial bank arrangements and IMF adjustment programs.

After having secured some official bridge financing, Mexico, following its presidential elections, implemented a series of severe austerity measures. Mexico's rapid development plans based on its oil revenues were sharply curtailed. Following a sharp devaluation of the peso, Mexico's government also took steps to limit public sector expenditures, restrain wages and reduce imports by, among other things, imposing a value-added tax. These measures improved Mexico's tarnished reputation for economic mismanagement, impressed its creditors, and repaired, in part, its creditworthiness.

Between 1982 and 1984, Mexico was touted as an example of a country undergoing a successful adjustment program, although critics pointed to the "lumping," that is, the bunching of maturities requiring massive refinancing, that Mexico would face in the mid- to late 1980s. Nonetheless, in mid-1985 Mexico succeeded in obtaining certain concessions from its international banks, and negotiated a multi-year rescheduling agreement at lower spreads. About $48 billion, or one-half of Mexico's total obligation, was rescheduled such that the repayment of principal was amortized until 1999 (see Figure 2.1). Ostensibly, Mexico was being rewarded with generous lending terms and a multi-year rescheduling agreement by the international banks for implementing a successful austerity program.[13]

By 1985 concern had surfaced about the slow pace of Mexico's recovery, the sharp drop in the standard of living, and the growing political pressures. Indeed, serious questions remain whether the Mexican austerity program has been successful and whether it is the appropriate model for other debtors to follow. Mexico has not increased its exports and its export performance has been largely determined by oil prices. The country's inflation rate has been significantly above the government's goal, its exchange rate policy has been criticized, government spending remains high, and unemployment has been rising despite a drop in real wages.[14] Indeed, Mexico's creditors have grown increasingly nervous about the country's announced intention of seeking additional loans and its requirements for massive reschedulings. Ironically, Mexico was declared ineligible for fur-

FIGURE 2.1. Mexico: Amortizations of Mexican Public Sector Debt to Commercial Banks Subject to Financing Principles

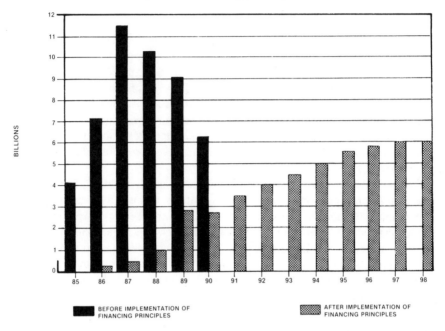

Note: This chart assumes a prepayment of U.S. $1 billion in 1984 of the outstandings under the 1983 $5 Billion Credit Agreement.

Source: The United Mexican States Financing Principles for Mexican Public Sector Debt to Commercial Banks Maturing 1985 to 1990 (September 8, 1984).

ther IMF drawings because of its failure to comply with its IMF program on the very day, September 19, 1985, an earthquake struck the country and caused an estimated $5 billion in damage.

Yet Mexico's case illustrates the usefulness of having the IMF play the "tough cop" role when the government is aware that certain steps must be taken. By being used as a government's "whipping boy," the IMF has also been used to divert domestic dissatisfaction from measures that a government views as necessary. As Mexico's finance minister expressed it: "It is recognized that the costs and sacrifices have been high and they have been reflected in a diminished standard of living for many Mexicans. But it is also certain that had this decision not been taken, the costs would have been higher and irreversible."[15]

Although the March 1985, $50 billion Mexican loan restructuring was hailed by some bankers as "the beginning of the end" of the debt crisis, Mexico's financial condition deteriorated rapidly toward the end of the year. The government's spending in anticipation of the 1985 midterm elections, the sharp drop in oil prices, and the impact of the September 1985 earthquakes aggravated Mexico's debt service problems. Its initial estimate of the need for additional new loans from its creditor banks and other sources was $10 billion over three years. However, the amount was revised several times reaching $6 to $10 billion for 1986 alone, with Mexican Finance Minister Silva Herzog explaining that $4 billion of additional new borrowing would be needed to finance a $6 billion capital gap.[16]

Mexico's President de la Madrid noted the country's severe foreign debt problem in a major policy address on February 22, 1986, in which he adopted a conciliatory tone but urged that the country's capacity to pay should be the standard for determining its debt service. Although he proposed that changes be made through negotiations, he served notice that his country would no longer accept permanent stagnation or austerity.[17] Yet Mexico's creditors are likely to insist on an austerity program and structural adjustments as a condition for providing additional financing.

Nevertheless, some bankers have expressed the view that U.S. proximity and national security interests with respect to Mexico may be used to justify treating it as a special case. Such a policy could result in a successful test case for the Baker Plan, even if that country's financing needs would consume nearly the entire proposed amount of funds.[18] Indeed, by August 1986 the United States was engaged in providing Mexico with a bridge loan as part of a $12 billion loan package outlined by Mexico and the IMF.

Brazil

Having built its development strategy on a policy of borrowing foreign exchange, Brazil, by the end of 1982, had a foreign debt obligation of over $90 billion, with $70 billion owed to commercial banks, $22 billion of that amount to U.S. banks. Brazil's debt-servicing obligation in 1983 amounted to about $24 billion, over $10 billion in interest payments alone, which represented about 120 percent of its exports, with total debt at about 360 percent of its exports. The burden of financing its imports and servicing its debts exceeded Brazil's export earnings despite that country's impressive and successful export development drive, which, in turn, has stirred certain protectionist sentiments in the United States. The precipitous drop in Brazil's credit rating was prompted by its problems in managing this $90 billion debt. The frightened reaction of its creditors, Brazil's procrastination in arguing that it didn't have a "Mexican problem," and its mounting $3 billion 1983 debt arrearages exacerbated the problem.

During the fall of 1982, Brazil was also provided with swap arrangements, with about $1.2 billion of ESF bridge financing tied to progress on IMF programs. Official assistance provided by the United States and others to Mexico and Brazil was in tandem with a series of negotiations between those countries and their creditor banks, with their requests from the banks totalling $20 billion and $8 billion respectively.[19]

Brazil imposed austerity measures to cut back on its imports and slow down the growth of its outstanding debts. The Brazilian government took measures to reduce the expansion of domestic credit, limited the availability of dollars to its citizens, and cut back on its domestic spending, including reduction in the indexing of wages to inflation. Brazil's currency depreciated by one-third in 1983. Despite its trade surplus (even though the value of its exports had dropped by 13 percent), Brazil found it difficult to service its outstanding loans. In the meantime, the Bank of International Settlements—despite having extended the time on Brazil's loan on a number of occasions—made it clear that the pressure was on Brazil to make the payments.[20]

In describing the late 1983 agreement between Brazil and the IMF, Samuel Johnson's characterization of second marriages has been invoked—a triumph of hope over experience. The on-again off-again IMF program for Brazil revolved around the IMF's extension of loans on condition that Brazil adopt a series of measures designed to bring its spending to manageable levels. This agreement would reestablish Brazil's creditworthiness and serve as the justification for additional commercial bank loans. Although agreement on a $28 billion restructuring of Brazil's debt, including $6.5 billion in new loans and various arrangements to strengthen interbank deposits, was concluded in January 1984, some critics feared that such loans were neither a solution to the problem nor effectively providing time because of the acrimony and uncertainty surrounding the negotiations.

When Brazil failed to fulfill its austerity program, the IMF and international banks stopped previously agreed upon disbursements of about $9 billion, an amount critical for covering Brazil's financing gap. Yet the issue was resolved a short time later. However, a number of economists have pointed out that these additional funds barely covered Brazil's external financing needs. The effort to cut imports, such as oil, as a means of preserving badly needed foreign exchange hampered efforts to increase exports. For example, coal shortages curtailed efforts to expand steel exports. Although Brazil has reported a trade surplus of about $6.5 billion for 1983, significantly up from the $780 million for 1982, some criticize these as inflated numbers generated with mirrors, ''all a bit surrealistic,'' in the words of a prominent Brazilian.[21]

Brazil's state-owned companies account for a substantial amount of its foreign debt obligations. Their projects, as some Brazilians joke, may be an indication that Brazil is the country of the future and always will be. Such mammoth projects as the Itaipu—the world's largest hydroelectric plant—were initiated during Brazil's ''miracle years'' of the 1960s and 1970s. Even though several of these projects may be justified by future savings, they have triggered sweeping and negative denunciations. ''The dollar-gobbling projects, some of which now stand idle for lack of funds, are an embarrassing reminder to Brazilians of their costly delusions of grandeur.''[22]

In addition, Brazil's inflation has been rampant, and its indexing system has made inflation more difficult to control. A symbolic struggle ensued between the government and its political opposition over passage of a wage law limiting wage adjustments to 80 percent of the rise of the cost of living. The political opposition viewed the measure as "too much of a sacrifice on an already desperate working class."[23]

Despite its continuing economic difficulties, Brazil's $12 billion trade surplus in 1984 has provided hope for those who believe economic growth will provide the means for resolving the debt problems of certain countries. Many Brazilians, however, question whether the sacrifices they have been making to repay their debts have been worth the effort. Although Brazil has managed to replenish $8 billion in foreign exchange reserves, others are wondering whether, in light of the drop in the 1985 trade surplus, Brazil can continue to generate the surpluses necessary to service its foreign debt. In addition, the IMF suspended Brazil's loan payments in early 1985 because of its failure to implement its IMF program, especially in cutting inflation, thereby holding up negotiations on a $45 billion multi-year rescheduling agreement with the commercial banks. The death of Brazil's president-elect in mid-1985 complicated the country's political condition and contributed to the uncertainty regarding its economic well-being at a time when the commercial banks were surprised by Brazil's likely request for new financing. In a July 1985 television address, President Sarney took a more confrontational posture toward Brazil's creditors. He complained about the banks' "exorbitant interest rates" and the IMF's "dogmatic intransigence" for insisting on an unnecessary recession. Although affirming Brazil's desire to meet its commitments, he underscored his view that the country's debt burden poses a risk to the flourishing of the new democratic regime and that increased social spending is critical.[24]

Brazil's 1986 anti-inflationary measures (without adhering to an IMF program, yet with the IMF's tacit approval) and robust 8 percent growth rate provided a positive environment for an agreement to restructure $31 billion of Brazil's debt. President Sarney's March 1986 program to fight inflation included a wage and price freeze and creation of a new currency, which reflected a need to combat Brazil's internal debt crisis. The international banks agreed to reduce the interest rate spreads on Brazil's loans from 2.125 percent to 1.125 percent, thereby saving Brazil about $320 million a year on its debt service obligations.[25] Indeed, by mid-1986 the international financial community seems to have regained confidence in Brazil's performance.

Argentina

Argentina's political problems and the cost of its Falklands adventure, perhaps even more than its purely economic and financial difficulties, have been making its lenders anxious since 1982. Argentina's experience in managing its prior debt crisis combined with its significant $3 billion trade surplus in 1983 had provided a basis for the guarded optimism initially expressed by a number of its creditors.

Argentina's political environment frightened U.S. and other bankers, many of whom have concluded that, "if there is a country that thinks it can try to get away with repudiation, it's Argentina."[26] Prior to the October 1983 elections to replace its discredited military regime, Argentina's financial picture was shaken by the actions of a judge who ordered the arrest and questioning of the country's central bank president about the debt rescheduling of the country's airline. Some observers viewed this act as an indication of the resentment against IMF austerity measures and foreign creditors.

On March 30, 1984 the United States and several Latin American debtor countries put together an eleventh-hour financial rescue package for Argentina. Conceived by Mexico's finance minister, Jesus Silva Herzog, the plan, heralded as "ingenious," provided Argentina with breathing room by enabling it to make its interest payments to the international banks. Indeed, critics charged that this was yet another example of a "big bank bailout" by the U.S. government because U.S. banks did not have to take a "hit," that is, reduce their quarterly earnings. Denying the charge, the U.S. Treasury defended the action as a constructive effort to assist Argentina's new democratic government maintain its creditworthiness, protect the international monetary system, and demonstrate concern in helping resolve Latin America's debt problems.[27]

The financial rescue package included loans totaling $300 million from Mexico, Venezuela, Brazil, and Colombia, $100 million at a low interest rate from 11 banks, and U.S. agreement to lend $300 million of ESF resources upon Argentina's agreement on a letter of intent with the IMF. Argentina also used $100 million of its foreign exchange reserve to pay interest it owed its creditor banks. Under the initial plan, the proceeds of the U.S. loan were to be used by Argentina to pay its Latin American creditors while funds from the IMF were to be used to repay the U.S. loan. In mid-June 1984, the United States refused to renew its commitment because Argentina had not reached agreement with the IMF and Argentina's Latin American creditors announced that they would not extend their loans beyond July 31, 1984.

Ironically, by becoming creditors for purposes of the Argentina package, the Latin American countries were placed in an uncomfortable position. Rather than joining to repudiate their debts, key Latin American debtors were assisting another debtor to pay its debt to the banks and in the process acquired an interest in ensuring that Argentina reach agreement with the IMF on an economic adjustment program. A former Venezuelan diplomat described his country's attitude as schizophrenic because Venezuela had been adamant in its refusal to turn to the IMF yet was now in a position of encouraging Argentina to do so.

Nevertheless, the key Latin American debtors were fearful of harmful consequences to their creditworthiness if Argentina's situation deteriorated into a confrontation with the international banks. As one observer noted, "Argentina and the banks were eyeball to eyeball and Mexico blinked." Having implemented a tough austerity program to ensure its creditworthiness, Mexico's motives were understandable—here put simply by one its financial officials: "We have a lot of incentive to convince the other nations to be cautious. We have suffered a lot to get where we are, and we don't want to see them upset it."[28]

The Argentina financial package may have contributed to demands made at the Cartagena conference. Even though the June 1984 Cartagena conference did not create a debtor's cartel, it did establish a formal consultative mechanism for debtors to negotiate with their creditors regarding concessions for repaying the debt.

Argentina's tortuous negotiations with the IMF reflected the difficulties associated with implementing an austerity program in light of severe economic problems and labor union demands. Argentina's protracted efforts to implement an IMF program have haunted Argentina's economy and creditworthiness, the international banks, and the international financial system. In December 1984, the United States agreed to extend a $500 million short-term loan to Argentina as part of an overall emergency financial package that included agreement with the IMF on a $1.6 loan. Argentina agreed to pay a substantial portion of its $1.2 billion interest arrears to its creditor banks, thereby allowing them to include about $850 million in 1984 earnings. The banks agreed to reschedule about $14 billion of Argentina's loans due by 1985 and to provide new loans of $4.2 billion, increasing their exposure to Argentina significantly.[29] Many bankers expressed skepticism over the likelihood that Argentina would stay in compliance with the IMF program and reestablish its creditworthiness. Others, however, suggested that the Argentina package represents a benchmark in the process toward an orderly resolution of the debt debacle.[30]

In March 1985 President Alfonsin warned the United States that the Latin American debt crisis posed a severe threat to peace and stability in the region.[31] Despite his harsh criticism of the IMF's conditions and the U.S. debt strategy, he later declared his willingness to pay the political price for imposing economic austerity policies.[32] On June 14, 1985 Argentina adopted a series of measures designed to combat its 30 percent per month inflation rate and introduced a new currency, the austral, to replace the peso. In addition, Argentina reached agreement with the IMF to reestablish its $1.2 billion loan, made a $250 million payment in overdue interest of about $1 billion, obtained a multilateral "bridge" loan of about $460 million, and negotiated the release of a $4.2 billion rescheduling package from its commercial banks.[33] In the assessment of one banking official: "Alfonsin is finally taking the bull by the horns. Whether he throws Argentina or Argentina throws him, we're just going to have to see."[34]

The turnaround in Argentina's prospects has been hailed by the international banking community. Indeed, Argentina has even replaced Mexico as the model debtor whose efforts could demonstrate a successful program for meeting its foreign debt payments.[35] Although Argentina did not follow the orthodox IMF approach for resolving its financial difficulties, its dramatic measures propelled it into the leading candidate as a successful test case for the Baker Plan. However, despite its renewed access to bank credits and an IMF standby agreement, Argentina has not, to date, agreed to serve as the model country for a Baker Plan loan.

Smaller Latin Debtors

Although the primary focus of the debt crisis has been on certain Latin American countries, especially Mexico, Brazil, and Argentina, in large part because of the substantial commercial bank exposure, other countries in the region are also plagued by a serious debt burden. Within Latin America, some countries have opted to adopt different courses of action. Venezuela, for example, has refused to turn to the IMF and has sought to manage its debt and creditworthiness by implementing its own economic measures. Indeed, in 1986 it succeeded in negotiating a $21.2 billion public sector rescheduling agreement with commercial banks based on implementation of its own economic adjustment program rather than the IMF's. Nevertheless, because of Venezuela's dependence on oil revenues, rapidly falling oil prices in 1986 may require a reopening of and substantial changes to the agreement. Countries such as Chile, Peru, and Bolivia are struggling with their debt burden and are experiencing a sense of helplessness over the sheer magnitude of their debt and inability to service it. In 1985 Peru's new president, Alan Garcia Perez, vowed to reject IMF austerity packages. Moreover, Peru's interest arrears to commercial banks have forced U.S. bank regulators to lower the country's creditworthiness classification, while Garcia proclaimed that Peru would limit its debt service to 10 percent of its exports. Bolivia declared a formal suspension of its debt payments in May 1984, Nigeria announced that its 1986 budget would limit foreign debt payments to 30 percent of its annual export revenue, others have not serviced their debts for prolonged periods, and many debtors have begun to be more assertive in demanding concessions from their bankers.

In view of its compliance with austerity measures demanded by the IMF, Chile, notwithstanding its political problems, has been viewed as a model borrower by international commercial banks. However, its lower export earnings combined with the reluctance of commercial banks to lend new money threaten to undercut the rationale and incentive for other countries to be model borrowers. Indeed, as a means of seeking to reward Chile for its economic efforts, Chile's loan package for 1985 includes a World Bank guarantee to commercial banks for an additional $400 million above the $780 million previously committed.[36] The bleak outlook of such smaller debtors as Senegal, Togo, the Ivory Coast, Bolivia, Peru, Jamaica, and Chile has been attributed to their lack of economic and political clout. Yet their combined loans are significant and their weariness from belt-tightening adjustment measures could set an example for other debtors to follow.[37]

Other Regions

In Asia the focus of international bankers has been on the Philippines' debt problem. The $38 billion South Korean debt burden, about $14 billion of it in short-term loans, is larger than that of the Philippines, but South Korea's credit-worthiness has remained strong because of its healthy economic base. Chronic economic difficulties have been confronting the Philippines since the 1970s. The seriousness of its $26 billion foreign debt servicing problems were exacerbated by the shaken confidence of international bankers, in reaction to the assassination of Ferdinand Marcos' opposition leader Benigno Aquino in August 1983. The political instability besetting the Philippines has dampened the enthusiasm of foreign bankers' willingness to pump additional funds into the country, although many bankers realize that they will have to lend more money to maintain the country's financial viability. These problems were compounded by the revelation that its central bank had been reporting $600 million more in reserves than it had as a means of trying to reassure foreign lenders, rather than reveal the capital flight following the Aquino assassination. Such reactions to these types of events underscore the importance of the psychological issue of confidence.

Severe economic problems facing the country and the reluctance of foreign lenders to increase their exposure have driven the Philippine government to agree with the IMF to impose austerity measures, despite the possibility of disenchantment by the populace. These measures were a precondition for an IMF loan, and may have to be accompanied by political steps necessary to restore the confidence of the international financial community.[38] In 1985, commercial banks agreed to provide the Philippines with a financing package of $925 million.

By 1986, the IMF economic adjustment program in the Philippines was in disarray in light of the turmoil surrounding the presidential elections and the ensuing events that resulted in the ouster of Ferdinand Marcos. President Corazon Aquino has inherited a financial problem of enormous magnitude and has sought the assistance of the international financial community.[39]

Numerous African countries are facing severe economic problems. Nigeria's government reacted to the rapid erosion of its oil revenues and budget finances by imposing increased import restrictions, thereby reducing imports by about one-third, depreciating its currency, and limiting its borrowing. The Nigerian oil boom that had generated annual revenues of $26 billion during the late 1970s generated only $10 billion in 1983, while its foreign debt rose to about $15 billion. As a result of rampant corruption and other political and economic strains, the democratic government was overthrown by military officers at the end of 1983. The new government took immediate steps to reassure its foreign creditors by continuing to make its payments and to negotiate with the IMF.

However the population problems and food shortages plaguing Nigeria, as well as the drought and famine afflicting several African countries, reveal the severe circumstances confronting the African continent. Food riots in Tunisia,

Morocco, Sudan and several other countries have strained their political systems.[40] In the Middle East, Egypt and Israel are also experiencing serious economic strains and foreign debt servicing problems.

In Eastern Europe, Poland's financial problems have been the most serious and led to a sharp curtailment of bank loans to other countries in the region. Poland's debt crisis emerged when government austerity measures triggered labor unrest and confrontations with Solidarity. The imposition of martial law sparked a Western reaction that included trade sanctions and refusal to proceed with debt rescheduling negotiations. Although Poland did not make repayments to its official creditors in 1982, the country was not declared in default, in large part because of the substantial exposure of European banks and U.S. government guarantees of U.S. loans. Yugoslavia also experienced a sharp cutback in its ability to generate loans from commercial banks in 1982 and required a rescue package in excess of $5 billion from the BIS and other international financial institutions. Other East European countries, such as Romania, Hungary, and East Germany, also have significant foreign debt burdens.

CAPITAL FLIGHT, DEBT REPAYMENT, AND IMPLICATIONS OF DEFAULT

Arguments have raged about how and whether the debts of these developing countries will be repaid. In part, the arguments center on whether the debt problem is to be viewed as a collection of funds by the commercial banks or their long-term commitment to the funding and growth of certain economies. Walter Wriston, former chairman of Citicorp, has suggested that fears of debtor countries' defaults or bankruptcies are misplaced. Pointing to the fact that countries do not disappear, he argues that the key factor for banks is whether debtor countries can make the interest payments, not whether the full amount of principal is ever repaid, which the banks never expected. Some of Wriston's banking colleagues have suggested otherwise, noting that the issue of creditworthiness hinges on those factors that "directly affect the soundness and eventual repayment of the underlying credit involved."[41] The applicable analogy, according to Wriston, is the U.S. Treasury's periodic new borrowings that fund its previous ones.[42]

Wriston's critics counter that the analogy is faulty, arguing that U.S. creditworthiness is based on its economic and political system and also pointing out the U.S. government's ability to generate dollars. Questions about these countries' creditworthiness—in large part because of the enormity of the foreign debts they are trying to service—are at the core of the problem. Wriston's harshest critics, calling him the "Peter Pan of bankers because he still believes in fairies," point out that even if countries do not disappear—and history has numerous examples of those that have—governments do change. Furthermore, countries as well as other debtors have stopped payments in the past and some have repudiated their foreign debts, as occurred during the 1930s, for example.[43]

The United Kingdom and France defaulted on their payments to the United States "on the grounds that their obligations to meet the needs of their people were greater than the obligations to creditors."[44] Several Latin American countries defaulted on their bonds in the nineteenth century as well as in the 1930s.[45]

Although many bankers viewed loans to foreign countries as essentially risk-free, critics such as George Champion, retired chairman of Chase Manhattan, have argued that they are extremely risky.

> There's no way you can collect when you lend to a foreign government. When you take somebody else's money and lend it to some organization over which you have no control, and there is no [secondary market], then you've transgressed the fundmentals of sound banking. Just because a country is in existence doesn't mean they're going to pay [their debts]. Secondly, there's no way to get a country to limit the amount of debt it incurs.[46]

In short, even if sovereign states do not go bankrupt, they can and do stop servicing their debts. Mexico's 1982 financial squeeze was exacerbated by its efforts to finance its deficits through borrowings of shorter maturities until it could no longer do so. Its solution was built on obtaining more liquidity in combination with an IMF program. If there is no money, nobody can be paid, although many key debtor countries had to borrow more to do so, a situation described as "turning matters inside-out."[47]

Capital flight out of these debtor countries has been serious and has exacerbated their debt problem.[48] The infusion of additional capital by creditor governments and private financial institutions into key debtor countries occurred while massive capital flight out of those countries was hemorrhaging their financial flows. In short, borrowed money was used to finance capital flight. Approximately $55 billion of capital fled from Latin America during the 1978–1983 period. Mexico experienced capital flight totalling $17 billion, Argentina $11 billion, and Venezuela $8 billion during 1981–1982. Not only did such capital flight increase these debtor countries' burden by about one-third, but it also raises a serious question regarding the rationale for pumping additional cash from foreign governments and banks into these countries as their citizens take their money out.[49] While the foreign debts are largely owed by governments, the capital flight went into financing foreign assets that are privately owned. Although debtor countries need to instill confidence to stem this outflow, the international banking community has been criticized for assisting in promoting capital flight, especially the approximately $130 billion from Latin America.[50]

The *Banamex* case presents an interesting example of Mexico's effort to limit the depletion of its foreign exchange. The devaluation of the Mexican peso occurred when the Mexican government stopped intervening in support of a stable price for the pseo. The Mexican government had done so between 1977 and 1982 but its liquidity crisis of 1982 prompted it to issue a decree that foreign currency accounts held in Mexican banks and payable in Mexico were to be paid only in pesos. Foreign currency accounts were to be automatically converted into pesos at the new prevailing exchange rate. This action prompted several law suits against Mexican banks. In the *Banamex* case, Wolf sought to recover the exchange losses he had incurred as a result of the devaluation of the peso and its impact on his dollar account which had been converted into pesos under the Mexican decree. Although Wolf succeeded in District Court in arguing that he was entitled to damages under the U.S. Securities Act because Banamex had sold unregistered securities, Banamex prevailed on appeal.[51]

Benjamin Weiner has suggested that the current global foreign debt will not be repaid and may simply be forgotten. Invoking as instructive the example of the way the U.S. Treasury Department handles debts owed by allies and enemies of the United States since World War I, he points out that despite the likelihood that these debts will not be collected, the U.S. Treasury Department continues to publish the principal and accrued interest of the debtors. Weiner argues that this episode demonstrates that no reprisal or chaos arose from the nonpayment of these debts, prompting him to suggest, whether facetiously or not is unclear, that the solution for the developing nations lies in promising to repay their debts immediately after the World War I debtors do likewise.[52] A serious deficiency in his point is that a substantial portion of this foreign debt is held by banks whose regulators have not been willing to allow these loans to be held on the banks' books indefinitely.

The argument has been made that commercial banks have been willing to provide new credits to the debtor countries by maintaining "the fiction that these credits will someday be repaid by increased exports."[53] New credits have been geared primarily to a debtor country's ability to service its higher interest payments. Accordingly, "betting on the future creditworthiness of these debtors may prove an expensive game."[54]

Even if a debt moratorium or default by major debtors would be an irrational act because of the drastic impact on their creditworthiness and their need for future access to capital markets, rationality may be a rare commodity if social and political pressures reach a boiling point in these countries. The importance of developing countries to the U.S. economy is reflected by the fact that these countries serve as a market for 38 percent of U.S. merchandise exports and 25 percent of U.S. foreign direct investment.[55]

Although the impact of a cessation of debt servicing by Brazil or Latin America as a whole on the U.S. and Western economies is difficult to predict and depends, in some measure, on how the Federal Reserve Board, other bank regulators, and other actors manage such a crisis, available projections clearly indicate the severe economic consequences to creditor countries of such an action. Data Resources Inc. estimated that in 1984 a debt moratorium by Brazil— with $90 billion of foreign debt and $22 billion owed to U.S. banks—would have caused a $25 billion drop in the U.S. gross national product and would have eliminated 400,000 jobs. With $71 billion then owed to U.S. banks, a concerted Latin American debt moratorium would, at a minimum, have sharply curtailed bank earnings and lowered its loan capacity. There was a possibility that leading banks could become insolvent and that the accompanying loss of confidence could shatter confidence in the financial system as a whole. In addition, the U.S. GNP would have fallen by $70 billion and 1.1 million Americans would have lost their jobs.[56]

Although most experts agree with Federal Reserve Chairman Paul Volcker's assessment that "we can handle even large isolated instances" of debt crises, critics charge that this view is based in large part on faith.[57] However, to the extent that the international financial community agrees with that assessment, the critical element of confidence can be maintained. Yet a debt moratorium or repudiation by a major debtor could set an example for other debtors to follow.

The nightmare of many international bankers and finance officials is that such a moratorium would spread throughout the international banking system. Their major fear is the uncertainty associated with the possible insolvency of major international banks with harrowing consequences for the banking system and the economics of debtor and creditor countries. Furthermore, it is not known how or whether a widespread debt moratorium would be managed. Even though progress has been made in coping with the debt crisis, these fears are reawakened periodically when debtor countries meet to discuss their options and possible concerted action.

Warnings have been raised about the dangers surrounding a series of reprisals by creditor governments and international banks, as well as counteractions by the debtors, with the particular scenario dependent on the country involved in the event of a repudiation.[58] Countries adopting a conciliatory default, such as a unilateral rescheduling formula as opposed to a repudiation, may provoke differing reactions by banks and regulators.[59] Rather than establishing formal institutions, it has been suggested that contingency plans be developed to grapple with the debt problem on a case-by-case basis, with negotiations as the means of coping with the major difficulties.[60] Whether future actions will be amenable to amicable negotiations, usually involving reschedulings, is the question that remains unanswered as major debtor countries require increased financing.

SOCIAL AND POLITICAL CONSTRAINTS ON THE DEBTORS

The reduction in the growth rates of developing countries during the early 1980s caused increased unemployment and brought to an abrupt halt much of the economic and social progress achieved by developing countries during the 1970s. The drop in economic wealth and the implementation of austerity measures have eroded living standards, and their greatest impact has been on portions of the population whose economic advancements occurred during the periods of dramatic growth. Unemployment, slow growth, and high inflation have undermined a nascent middle class in many of the debtor countries. The weakening of this class undercuts the basis for political stability and contributes to political polarization.[61] In several countries those disaffected by the loss of their recent economic gains joined those at or near the poverty level to take part in protests, riots, and raids on supermarkets.

Many experts feared that prolonged austerity measures adopted as part of the 1983 IMF programs and rescheduling efforts would result in debt repudiation, riots, or even revolution. They believed governments of developing countries would opt for measures to avoid these consequences. In short, certain governments confronting social unrest and severe unemployment might prefer to limit or even eliminate payments to their international creditors. In Brazil, for example, in 1983 support began to mount for declaring a moratorium forcing a debt renegotiation, including a grace period, longer terms and reduced interest rates.[62]

Although some economic adjustment efforts have resulted in social and political strains in several countries, the dire consequences predicted by many critics have not been borne out to date.[63] Indeed, many debtor countries have exhibited a surprising degree of social and political resilience. The chances for the success of austerity programs would appear to require fine tuning to avoid causing social upheaval if the measures are too tough, or a cutback of foreign commercial loans if they are not tough enough. Some have argued that IMF resources have made adjustment easier and decreased the chances of political instability. Nonetheless, "IMF programs do expose elites to charges of selling the sovereignty of their countries."[64] Mindful of the fragility inherent in the austerity approach, a number of leading figures from developing countries, including President Alfonsin and President Sarney, have launched harsh attacks on the prescription of adjustment measures the IMF has been urging on them.[65]

> If re-entrenchment goes too far, it will probably bring on a revolt and a takeover by a nationalistic regime that would repudiate Brazil's foreign debt. If it doesn't go far enough—as appears likely—foreign banks will find it difficult to put up the money Brazil will need over the next several years. In that case, too, Brazil is probably in for dangerous social turbulence.[66]

As austerity measures, such as cutting wages, are implemented, they can trigger social and economic dislocations with potentially severe political consequences. For example, the Dominican Republic experienced some 55 deaths in riots protesting IMF austerity programs. Austerity measures contributed to the overthrow of President Nimeiri of Sudan in 1985. Indeed, this is one of the few cases of such a causal relationship. Even though conditionality has been associated with political instability, the instability was associated with the overall economic situation and not specifically to the IMF program. Jamaica has experienced protests and even Brazil has witnessed unrest which, although sporadic, has underscored the fragile balance as a government seeks to enforce cutbacks without sparking political unrest.

> While government officials, the IMF, politicians and businessmen grapple with the targets and statistics of austerity, the Brazilian masses live it. During the past three years, real per capita income in Brazil has fallen more sharply than during the Depression of the 1930's. More than a quarter of Brazil's work force of 49 million is either out of work or "underemployed," meaning that the family head cannot even earn a $66 minimum monthly wage. The slums that millions of Brazilians live in were beginning to improve, but with austerity the construction of sewage systems, hospitals, and schools has come to a standstill. In desperation a traditionally peace-loving and resilient people have taken to crime. Some 230 riots and lootings were reported in September [1983] alone. In a country where hope has been nurtured by an unflappable faith in a superpower future, little hope remains.[67]

Implementation of such austerity measures requires a high degree of political tolerance in these financially strapped developing countries as time is needed for the necessary adjustments to occur. As serious questions are raised regarding the effectiveness of these measures, debtor countries are likely to insist on assured prospects of economic growth that will generate foreign earnings greater than their interest payments. Otherwise, they will have little incentive to continue such austerity measures and debt servicing. Equally ominous is the spreading perception among debtor countries that they are bearing the brunt of the sacrifices so that the commercial banks will not have to recognize losses. Ranging from demonstrations in Sudan with cries of "We will not be ruled by the IMF," slogans in Argentina of "Don't pay the IMF with the hunger of the people," and posters in Mexico protesting the high debt burden to U.S. banks, the cries of the debtor countries may be muted but the outlines of the complaint are clear.[68] The unanswered question is whether (and for how long) the political stability in these countries will hold as the austerity measures induce social and political strains.

> Time is needed, for the austerity measures cannot be too harsh, or they will not work and they will not be credible. It is essential that the austerity measures be distributed fairly across social groups, not that those who have benefited the least from previous excesses also be the ones asked to pay most of the price. Belt tightening where it is no longer possible can only jeopardize existing political and social structures. It could lead to political and social upheaval with consequences far more dramatic than any prospect of bank failures or country defaults.[69]

The rise to power of a political leader in a key debtor country interested in ceasing or unilaterally limiting the repayment of foreign debt obligations holds the potential not only for setting a precedent for other leaders in a similar position, but also for causing a series of reprisals by creditor countries. Creditor countries are sensitive to their national security interests in insuring that the pressures in debtor countries do not spread and generate social and political instability. For example, the United States has important security interest in key debtor countries and has sought to ensure that U.S. relations with them not become adversarial. Indeed, the goal of maintaining key debtor countries afloat by urging banks to generate additional loans may have prevailed over concern about the high exposure levels of U.S. banks.[70] Yet the unanswered question remains whether it is realistic to expect that the world's developing countries, even though they did hire the money, will continue to work in order to transfer more capital to their creditors than they receive. A social and political explosion sparked by the debt problem has not occurred to date, but the sacrifices made by debtor countries have been based on the assumption that these austerity programs would be temporary. As debtor countries become weary of continuing belt-tightening policies in effect since 1982, a dangerous element of cynicism may result as the temptation rises to look for an "easy way out."

DEBTORS' CARTEL

Some developing countries have reacted to the contraction of commercial bank credit, and the fact that since 1982 their debt service payments have been greater then the new loans they received, by considering unilateral moratoriums on debt service or even debt repudiation. Walter Wriston has suggested that "they would be cutting off their source of funds. They would be cutting their own throat by setting up a cartel."[71]

Mexico reportedly considered repudiating its foreign debts and approached both Brazil and Argentina at the height of its debt crisis during the summer of 1982 to form a debtors' cartel.[72] From time to time, international commercial banks and the industrial countries have been concerned that debtor countries would try to organize a debtor cartel, a move some feared would emerge from the September 5, 1983 Caracas ministerial conference on external financing and the June 1984 Cartagena meetings. Arguably, developing countries, especially key Latin American states, would use such a cartel to bargain with their creditors to obtain better terms and larger amounts of loans.

In large measure, the realization of a debtor's cartel has been aborted by differing interests of leading countries at key junctures. Nevertheless, the Cartagena meetings did reach agreement on creation of a debtors' consultative mechanism and demands for better credit terms, moves approaching the creation of a debtors' cartel. Participants of the Cartagena meetings agreed to seek a meeting with the industrial countries in order to search for ways to solve the debt crisis, although many debtor countries emphasized that they would continue to negotiate with international banks on improved loan terms.[73] Debtor countries have also been encouraged by the willingness of industrialized countries to discuss the debt problem within the framework of international financial institutions. Fears that such meetings may raise debtors' expectations for financial concessions unacceptable to the creditors have given way to assessments that no serious global negotiations will take place.

Although not interested in joining a debtor's cartel in 1982 because of its need for additional financing, Brazil has since then had to make severe domestic adjustments to conform to a proposed IMF program. Pressures accompanying the adoption of these measures generated a substantial amount of anti-IMF feeling in Brazil. With increasing frequency, Brazilian cries were heard in favor of imposing a unilateral moratorium on its debt service. Even if Brazil might have found the formation of such a debtor cartel more appealing during its arduous negotiations with the IMF, Mexico, having shored up its creditworthiness and reestablished its access to international capital markets, was less willing to undertake measures that would make its creditors nervous.

The idea of a debtors' cartel may be difficult to implement because it has not been able to take into account the uniqueness of each debtor's specific conditions and the need for the continued involvement of commercial banks and governments.[74] Indeed, at the June 1984 Cartegena meetings Mexico and Brazil reportedly assured that a debtor's cartel not be created. Some Latin American countries attributed this position to the multi-year financing at reduced spreads Mexico had received from the international banks shortly before those meetings convened, an offer also considered for Brazil. Charges were made that this was an effort by the international banks to divide and conquer the debtors, while Jacques de Larosiere and others suggested and defended the action as a means of rewarding those countries making the IMF-supported adjustment efforts.

In the December 1985 Cartagena Group's "Declaration of Montevideo" the debtor countries reviewed the Baker Plan as a positive but insufficient step. They believe the Baker Plan represents the politicization of the debt crisis since it launches a political dialogue. The debtors also adopted a more confrontational approach toward their creditors by arguing that a debtor country should "limit its net transfers of resources to avoid a greater social and political instability which would reverse the process of democratic consolidation."[75] In their emergency plan, the debtors included such proposals as a sharp decline in real interest rates, a link between debt service and resources needed for a country's economic growth, increased bank lending, and separation of old and new loans such that concessions are granted on old loans but regular terms are maintained for new loans.

Periodic meetings of certain debtor countries, such as the Cartagena conferences, have revealed their common concern over certain specific items but also some of their divergent interests. Nevertheless, these meetings tend to undercut confidence for the eventual cooperative resolution of the issue, make international bankers nervous, serve to signal the political significance of the debt crisis, and reflect what the data also reveal in stark terms, namely the vulnerability of debtor countries and international banks to each others' actions.

NOTES

1. Pedro-Pablo Kuczynski, "Latin American Debt," *Foreign Affairs,* Winter 1982/83, p. 344, and "Latin American Debt: Act Two," *Foreign Affairs,* Fall 1983, p. 17.

2. Takeshi Watanabe, Jacques Lesourne, and Robert S. McNamara, *Facilitating Development in a Changing Third World* (New York: The Trilateral Commission, 1983), p. 11.

3. Robert D. Hormats, "The Outlook for the Developing Country Debt Problem," Washington, D.C.: The Joint Economic Committee, June 24, 1985.

4. Watanabe, et al., op. cit., p. 12.

5. Ibid., p. 8.

6. Fritz Leutwiler, "International Indebtedness and World Trade," Philadelphia: Fifth International Monetary and Trade Conference, December 4, 1983, p. 3.

7. R.T. McNamar, "The International Debt Problem: Working out a Solution" (Philadelphia, Pa.: Fifth International Monetary and Trade Conference, December 5, 1983), p. 5.

8. *Time,* "The Debt-Bomb Threat," January 10, 1983.

9. McNamar, op. cit., p. 4.

10. Edward L. Mercaldo, "Mexico: One Country's Attempt at Dealing with the International Liquidity Crisis," *The World of Banking,* March-April 1984.

11. For a somewhat controversial account of those events, see Joseph Kraft, *The Mexican Rescue* (New York: Group of Thirty, 1984).

12. McNamar, op. cit., p. 4.

13. *Business Week,* "Will Mexico Make It?" October 11, 1984, p. 74.

14. *The Economist,* "Mexico Fails to Pass Politics, Philosophy, and Economics," May 18, 1985, p. 71.

15. As quoted in Richard Meislin, "Some Worries Emerge on Mexico's Progress," The New York *Times,* July 23, 1984.

16. Steve Frazier, "How Mexico, Once Model Debtor Nation, Sank into State of Economic Crisis," *The Wall Street Journal,* December 4, 1985; "Mexican Debt," *The Economist,* March 22, 1986.

17. *Foreign Broadcast Information Service,* "Mexico: De La Madrid Speech on Economic Situation," February 22, 1986.

18. *The Economist,* "Mexico Sends Baker's Plan back to the Drawing-Room," February 8, 1986.

19. See M.S. Mendelsohn, *Commercial Banks and the Restructuring of Cross-Border Debt* (New York: Group of Thirty, 1983).

20. *Institutional Investor,* "Country Credit Ratings," September 1983, p. 248.

21. As quoted in Edward Boyer, "Why Lenders Should Still Be Scared," *Fortune,* December 12, 1983, p. 116, from which much of this information is derived.

22. Ibid., p. 124.

23. As quoted in ibid., p. 128.

24. Richard House, "Brazil's Sarney Publicly Attacks Creditors, IMF," The Washington *Post,* July 24, 1985.

25. *The Economist,* "Spread a Little Thinner," March 8, 1986.

26. *Business Week,* "Argentina Fires a Shot in the Debtor's Revolt," October 17, 1983, p. 47.

27. See Statement of David C. Mulford, assistant secretary of the Treasury for International Affairs, before the Subcommittee on International Trade, Investment and Monetary Policy of the Committee on Banking, Finance, and Urban Affairs, U.S. House of Representatives, May 1, 1984.

28. *The Wall Street Journal*, "Argentina Debt Pact Avoids Trouble Now, May Cause Pain Later," April 2, 1984.

29. Art Pine, "Argentina Gets Loan from IMF of $1.66 Billion," *The Wall Street Journal*, December 31, 1984, p. 12.

30. Rimmer de Vries as quoted in Clyde Farnsworth, "IMF Approves $20 Billion Aid For Argentina," The New York *Times*, December 29, 1984.

31. Clyde Farnsworth, "Argentina Warns Congress about Debt Crisis," The New York *Times*, March 21, 1985.

32. Jackson Diehl, "Economic Plan Questioned," The Washington *Post*, June 9, 1985.

33. Gordon Matthews, "Following Bank Holiday, Argentina Seems More Serious about Reform," *The American Banker*, June 17, 1985.

34. As quoted in *Newsweek*, "Betting the Democracy," June 24, 1985.

35. Everett G. Martin, "Argentina, Once Cast as an Errant Debtor Now Is Widely Hailed," *The Wall Street Journal*, December 4, 1985.

36. *Newsweek*, "New Twist in Debt Crisis," June 17, 1985.

37. Christine A. Bogdanowicz-Bindert, "Small Debtors: The Smouldering Crisis and U.S. Interest in an Orderly Solution," Washington, D.C.: House Subcommittee on International Development Institutions and Finance, June 27, 1985.

38. James L. Rowe, Jr., "Philippines Faces Foreign Debt Crisis," The Washington *Post*, December 25, 1983, p. F-1.

39. Peter Montagnon, "Hopes Pinned on Baker Initiative," *Financial Times*, March 17, 1986.

40. *Time*, "The Light That Failed," January 16, 1984, p. 24.

41. Harry Taylor and David Pflug, "The Overall Role of the International Banker and Key Considerations in Lending," in William H. Baughn and Donald R. Mandich (eds.), *The International Banking Handbook* (Homewood, Illinois: Dow-Jones-Irwin, 1983).

42. *Time*, "The Debt-Bomb Threat," January 10, 1983, p. 50.

43. Ibid.

44. As quoted in Christine A. Bogdanowicz-Bindert, "World Debt: The United States Reconsiders," *Foreign Affairs*, Winter 1985/86.

45. Ibid. See also Edgar Turlington, *Mexico and Her Foreign Creditors* (New York: Columbia University Press, 1930).

46. *Business Week*, "Citibank's Pervasive Influence on International Lending," May 16, 1983, p. 125.

47. Richard Coulson, "Banks at the Brink," *National Review*, February 18, 1983, p. 175.

48. As pointed out by Alexandre Lamfalussy of the BIS; see *The American Banker*, "Some Recent Latin Debt Was Fleeing," June 19, 1984.

49. William R. Cline, *International Debt and the Stability of the World Economy* (Washington, D.C.: Institute for International Economics, 1983), pp. 27–28.

50. Karin Lissakers, "Halt Those Bankers Using Getaway Cars," The New York *Times*, March 6, 1986.

51. *Wolf v. Banco Nacional de Mexico*, 549 F. Supp. 841 (N.D. Cal. 1982).

52. Benjamin Weiner, "When We Forgave (or Forgot) Our Debtors, " *The Wall Street Journal*, December 6, 1983.

53. Bogdanowicz-Bindert, op. cit.

54. Ibid.

55. Watanabe et al., op. cit., p. 111.

56. *Business Week*, "How an LDC Default Would Hit the U.S. Economy," November 7, 1983, p. 118.

57. Ibid.

58. Cline, op. cit., p. 91.

59. Anatole Kaletsky, *The Costs of Default* (New York: Priority Press, 1985).

60. Cline, op. cit.

61. Robert D. Hormats, "The Outlook for the Developing Country Debt Problem," Washington, D.C., Joint Economic Committee, June 24, 1985.

62. Linda Sandler, "Is Discounting Sovereign Debt the Way Out?" *Institutional Investor*, July 1983, p. 74.

63. Henry S. Bienen and Mark Gersovitz, "Economic Stabilization, Conditionality, and Political Stability," *International Organization*, Autumn 1985.

64. Ibid.

65. *Euromoney*, "The IMF vs. The People," October 1983, p. 90.

66. Boyer, op. cit., p. 128.

67. Ibid., p. 116.

68. As quoted in *Time*, "Fresh Fears about Mounting Debts," April 29, 1985, p. 62. Lydia Chavez, "Argentina Shaken by Bank Failures," The New York *Times*, May 13, 1985, pp. 1–10, and witnessed by one of the authors on a trip to Latin America in May 1985.

69. Leutwiler, op. cit., pp. 9–10.

70. Benjamin J. Cohen, "International Debt and Linkage Strategies: Some Foreign-Policy Implications for the United States," *International Organization*, Autumn 1985.

71. As quoted in *Time*, "A Prickly Dilemma for the Banks," June 18, 1984.

72. *The Banker*, "Latin American Debt," September 1983, p. 86.

73. See *The World Bank Annual Report* 1984, Washington, D.C.: The World Bank, 1984.

74. McNamar, op. cit., p. 7

75. *Ministerial Meeting of the Cartagena Consensus Debtors' Group*, "Declaration of Montevideo," December 17, 1986.

3

The Vulnerability
of the Lenders

Although a great deal of attention has been paid to the plight of debtor developing countries in light of their heavy debt service burden, the sheer size of
their debt has provided them with a potentially substantial degree of leverage over
their lenders and exposed the vulnerability of major international banks. Lord
Keynes is reported to have observed that, "If you owe the bank 100 pounds,
you are in trouble. If you owe the bank 1,000 pounds, the bank is in trouble."
The accuracy of the observation is reflected in the following hypothetical esti-
mate: if Brazil, Argentina, and Mexico were to miss one year's principal and
interest, a loss of $14 billion, their banks' average earnings of $4.5 billion would
be severely affected and the banks' combined $27 billion capital base would be
cut in half.[1] In short, an iron law of banking—"you will only be as good as
your customers"—has been reinforced.[2] The recent slow growth of the debtor
countries and the uncertainty surrounding their economic well-being have cast a
pall over the international banking and financial system.

CREDITWORTHINESS AND THE
RISE OF INTERNATIONAL LENDING

During the 1970–1982 period, international bank lending expanded twelve-
fold as the inflow of "petrodollar" deposits stimulated a search for additional
borrowers. Banks in creditor countries doubled the percentage—from 8.7 percent in 1973 to 17.4 percent in 1981—that international lending claims
represented.[3] Over one-half of such lending has been among developed countries, but a dramatic increase in loans to key developing countries was a major
feature of the post-1974 period.[4] During the 1970s this borrowing was encouraged by major banks that were in competition to generate more loans.[5] A

33

go-go banking mentality and the strong influence of certain key banks on the syndicated loan markets caused leaders of other banks to ignore the advice of their analysts to cut back their international lending in favor of assurances by leading bankers that there was no problem with foreign loans. This period has been described as the heyday of international lending, with charges that there was a binge on the part of international loan officers and the executive committees who approved these loans at the banks' headquarters. International banks shifted their lending activities from traditional project financing, based on evaluation of its prospects, to balance-of-payments financing. By 1985 the international banks had approximately $550 billion in loans outstanding to developing countries, with exposure to both their governments and companies located there. Interest payments were about $75 billion and total debt service before reschedulings were about $140 billion.[6]

Many leading U.S. banks have been generating well over one-half of their loans and profits from their international operations, with a significant portion derived from developing countries. For example, in 1982 Citibank generated about 20 percent of its earnings from its operations in Brazil. U.S. banks hold about one-half of the $360 billion owed to banks by Latin American countries as of 1985. Among the causes for this growth in international lending are the liquidity provided by petrodollar deposits; past interest rate ceilings on U.S. domestic loans; credit demand in the international arena by sovereign borrowers, local firms, and multinational corporations; competition among banks for greater market shares; the "follow the leader" banking syndrome; and often the lack of sufficient information and occasional misperceptions of the risks associated with such lending. Since international banks were in competition, despite their participation in syndicated loans, there was a lack of information regarding the total debt being accumulated by the borrowing countries. Although the growth in the exposure of individual banks attracted the attention of bankers and bank regulators, its significance was not fully appreciated until the advent of the 1982 debt crisis. In short, not only did regulatory agencies have a difficult role in trying to control such international bank lending, but international banks were unable to control the total borrowings of the debtor countries.

Not only did many developing countries borrow directly from banks, but they often guaranteed borrowings by private parties within their borders. Some bankers have suggested that during the 1970s the U.S. government not only encouraged the development of petrodollar recycling but that it assured U.S. banks that these loans were safe. Certain U.S. government agencies did issue guarantees for certain types of loans, but there does not appear to be a basis for the argument that the U.S. government issued an implicit guarantee for international lending, notwithstanding its encouragement of the process. Although many leading banks took great comfort from the guarantees provided by the governments of key debtor countries, the inability of such governments to generate hard currencies to service their debts during the post-1982 debt crunch would appear to have rendered some of these guarantees illusory. Indeed, loans to sovereign borrowers, thought by some bankers to be risk-free and lucrative given the interest rates charged, proved to have a significant element of risk.

Recycling of petrodollars was facilitated by the development of the syndicated loan market and expanded international lending. A syndicated international loan may include hundreds of banks that join to lend billions of dollars. By spreading the risk and allowing smaller lenders, especially many U.S. regional banks, to have access to the credit judgments and marketing capabilities of the larger banks, syndicated lending has played a significant role in raising funds for many key debtor countries.[7]

> With the emergence of syndicated loans as a major vehicle for cross-border lending, very large financing packages could be put together for individual countries with the loan loss risk being spread over a large number of banks. The use of syndications also drew many medium-sized banks into lending to developing countries for the first time....[8]

Although many banks were cognizant of the virtues and requirements of diversification, prudence, and safety as a response to risks posed by country concentration and high loan exposure, their lending activities in response to tempting opportunities placed them in an extremely vulnerable position by the early 1980s.[9] Although considered unlikely to occur, the combination of such factors as the downturn of the international economy and high real interest rates adversely affected the major debtor developing countries simultaneously. In the early development of international lending, the creditworthiness of countries that borrowed heavily from private banks—countries such as Brazil, Mexico, Argentina, Peru, Venezuela, the Philippines, Indonesia, and South Korea—emerged as an important issue. International banks and their country risk analysts stressed that obtaining new loans was a function of a country's maintenance of a good debt-servicing record, sound economic management, and its economic and financial prospects. Nonetheless, the new role of leading private banks as major sources of external financing to the biggest debtors raised questions about the appropriateness of such lending activities.[10] The uncertainty surrounding potential losses accompanying such international lending underscored the importance of assuring the safety of the banking system and has eroded the critical ingredient of confidence. "From a general viewpoint, there is an obvious need to ensure the financial soundness of private banks because of the essential role they play in a modern economy, and more particularly because of what it means for holders of banks deposits, investors in bank shares and individuals and firms who rely on the banks to finance their activities."[11]

Irving Friedman, then with Citibank, served as a leading proponent and often provided the intellectual basis for increased international lending. Proponents of international lending to developing countries pointed out that their balance-of-payments deficits could only be financed by inflows of loans, investment capital, or aid from external sources. They argued that certain developing countries—in particular, Mexico, Brazil, and Argentina—had "achieved the status of creditworthiness for substantial borrowing from private banks," that whatever problems did exist were manageable, and that this private lending had aided these creditworthy countries in their adjustment to the 1974 oil shock.[12] In 1976, when developing countries' debt stood at $70 billion, many proponents of international lending belittled the possibility that private banks would lose their freedom of action in making prudent lending decisions.[13] Some argued that the major banks could simply stop lending if problems arose. Cognizant of commercial banks' new role in providing almost half of developing country external financing by 1975, Friedman argued that "the private bank is on its own, deciding country risk and taking full responsibility for it, and fully aware that errors in judgment could adversely affect the bank's earnings stream and beyond that its reserves and capital."[14]

Advocates of international lending pointed to the attractiveness of the higher spreads on international loans than for domestic loans and suggested that the infusion of petrodollars made such recycling necessary and appropriate under the circumstances. Although commercial interest rates paid by developing countries for foreign-currency loans fluctuated considerably, by 1976 they were usually 1 to 2.25 percent above the London Interbank Offered Rate (LIBOR), the rate offered for deposits of a given currency and maturity in the London market by, or to, prime banks. Since interest rates charged by a lender are also intended to reflect the perceived risk of the borrower's ability and willingness to service the loan, the similarity of the interest rates charged developing countries with those of developed countries by the late 1970s was often used to support the contention that the risks associated with loans to developing countries were no greater than for loans granted to other creditworthy borrowers.

Critics of international lending to developing countries questioned whether loans made by commercial banks to finance such deficits make sense if the borrowing country does not or cannot generate income with which to repay the debt.[15] They argued that the international banks "would be compelled to roll over or renew loans made to borrowers in weak countries because they cannot risk the consequences of serious declines or cessations of lending."[16] They charged that loan risk standards for developing countries were lowered, warned about the possibility of repudiation or moratoriums by borrowing developing countries, questioned the availability of sufficient bank capital and reserves to meet such contingencies, and pointed out that the U.S. banking system was being placed in a vulnerable position because of overseas lending activities of private banks. Country risk analysts often overlooked the possibility that rapidly increasing bank exposure in several key developing countries with simultaneous debt service problems would place leading U.S. money centers in a vulnerable position and shake confidence in the viability of the banking system. Indeed, some even viewed the rising concentration and exposure as a positive development. "The process of commercial lending to the developing world—which remains only a fraction of international loans and total loans—has become concentrated among lenders and borrowers. It is encouraging that these transactions involve well-capitalized, sophisticated lenders and borrowers who have the organization and management to utilize the resources productively."[17]

Nonetheless, there was recognition of the dangers inherent in the rush into international lending even by its most ardent supporters. "It is essential that the private banks' credit standards not be lowered in the growth of such lending. It cannot be repeated too often that the private banks must maintain selectivity among borrowers and be guided by the actuarial principle of spreading of risk and avoidance of concentration."[18]

Bankers realized that foreign commercial and sovereign borrowers might delay the servicing of their cross-border loans or that a government might even repudiate its foreign financial obligations. They often concluded that such actions by individual borrowers would be manageable and the impact on capital and reserves would be limited to impairing profits in a particular year. A "worldwide 'holocaust' scenario with worldwide losses and write-offs that produces loss numbers that threaten the financial viability of the private banking system" was considered worrisome but unlikely to occur.[19] However, as early as 1978 some advocates of increased international lending were already cautioning about the vulnerability of major banks from loans to debtor countries whose debt service to export ratio then stood at over 20 percent. "Debt service maturities need to be carefully watched and efforts made to keep track of public and private borrowings to avoid a potentially embarrassing convergence of maturing obligations in excess of immediately available resources."[20]

Even though international banks had emphasized the development of country risk early warning systems to cope with the perils associated with their rising loan exposure, the financial squeeze of 1982 and its consequences raised questions about the value of such early warning systems. This was particularly apparent where a bank already had a substantial stake in a country and was presented with the stark choice of the lender's dilemma, that is, losing what it already had exposed or providing additional funds in the hopes that the country would be able to improve its economy and service both the outstanding loans and the new infusion of capital.

COUNTRY RISK ANALYSIS

Country risk analysis has focused on a bank's overall exposure in a given country stemming from loans to local borrowers. Country risk is the exposure to loss caused by events in a country as a result of "lending to an entity [government, public or private sector] in a foreign country in a currency other than the local one.''[21] Sovereign risk is a significant aspect of country risk and focuses on the ability of the government and its agencies to service or repay a loan, a development of particular concern given the public sector and balance of payments financing by international banks.

Through probability analysis used to calculate the likelihood of loss, country risk analysis usually focuses on a series of political, social, and economic factors. In the first category are such causes as war, riots, and political polarization; in the second are religious divisions and social antagonisms; in the third are labor strikes, sudden economic dislocations, and deterioration in GNP growth.[22] Since banking regulatory agencies evaluate a bank's country risk assessment method in relation to its amount and type of international exposure, banks have a virtual requirement, in addition to an incentive to safeguard their exposure, to undertake sophisticated country risk analysis.[23]

Commercial banks have split in their preference for country risk approaches (quantitative versus qualitative, or objective versus subjective). These differences are reflected in the methods used by *Institutional Investor* and *Euromoney* to initiate their country risk ratings.[24] Reacting to observations by bankers that loan margins were not adequately reflecting country risk, *Institutional Investor* periodically surveys international bankers to rate individual country creditworthiness. *Euromoney* bases its country risk rating or ranking on terms and conditions provided sovereign borrowers that used the syndicated loan market.

Banking critics of the utility of quantitative methods for country risk assessment have argued that statistical techniques and models have a built-in assumption that analysis of past occurrences can be used to forecast future events. One observer has commented that ''The final assessment of country risk involves a mixture of economic, political and legal factors and it is doubtful if there is much point in trying to set up a formal statistical process by which all these factors are summed to produce a single number.''[25]

During the 1970s a number of major banks opted to focus their efforts on country risk management rather than try to reduce country risk to a number. Different risk management approaches adopted by major commercial banks have sought to take advantage of corporate opportunities while avoiding threats. Many international banks, such as Chase Manhattan, established procedures for the banks' country officers to gather and discuss the advantages and disadvantages of a proposal. The contrasting views are resolved by a country risk committee composed of representatives from senior levels of the bank's divisions. This country risk committee also establishes the guidelines for the limits of the bank's exposure in specific countries. Chase Manhattan also developed an early warning system of management information and control networks staffed around the clock by senior bankers, international economists, and political analysts to monitor rapidly changing situations.

Citibank implemented ''a combination of portfolio management and country risk'' program based on its relevance and practical value to the bank's business.[26] Participants in this process have observed that "the discussion was never about an abstraction called country risk. It was about whether Citibank would be prepared to have $300 million of exposure with this maturity breakdown and this usage in this country."[27] Bank of America's overall country risk rating is based on a numerical score, but unlike many other banks, each analyst's qualitative political assessment is not transformed into a number. Chemical Bank has adopted a "special sheet method for looking at politics" that requires an analysis of a country's major political issues and actors.[28] Bankers Trust's evaluation aims at dividing the world into those countries that present significant opportunities versus those that have a dangerous environment for business.

European bankers have tended to reject the quantitative methodology in vogue with many American banks. Even though the overreliance on contacts and consultants by European banks is open to criticism, the country-by-country risk approach used by U.S. banks has "resulted in over-concentration on certain regions or certain sectors," especially in Latin America and the Middle East.[29] European and Japanese banks were more conservative in their international lending activities during the 1970s and have generally been more responsive toward extending grace periods and multi-year restructuring arrangements. Their more flexible attitude toward country risk may stem from their smaller exposure to debtor countries and the regulatory policies prevalent in many European countries that encourage the creation of loan loss reserves.

As certain developing countries turned to private banks to finance their growth and development, they had an incentive to establish their creditworthiness to gain access to the private capital markets. Perceived as strong borrowers, these governments often used their flexibility to finance inefficient state-run enterprises and subsidize domestic programs. It is unclear whether the lenders were fully aware how these loans were being used. Bank analysts often assumed that these countries' growing economies and exports would allow them to maintain a balance between their external debt service obligations and other demands for foreign exchange.

Until shortly before the 1982 debt crisis, many bank analysts continued to maintain the view that no debt crisis would occur because key debtors could finance their debts from increasing export revenues.[30] Indeed, this conclusion was predicated on an assumption thus far proven to be realistic, namely that "private banks will respond positively to demand for credit from creditworthy countries."[31] Ironically, although certainly not a novel occurrence, too much borrowing, often based on inadequate information available to commercial banks as well as debtor countries with respect to their outstanding obligations, combined with systemic risk, that is, negative developments unfolding on a global basis, contributed to the severity of the debt burden and became a major factor in the erosion of debtor countries' creditworthiness.

Although much of the international lending process has been driven by the demand of borrowing countries and entities, the lenders had to decide the amount and terms of the loans. The purpose of country risk monitoring was to manage and avoid exposure that banks regarded as unacceptable. "The creditworthiness of the individual borrower is decided on the basis of the normal credit criteria."[32] However, "no bank can delegate to an outside body the responsibility for judging a country from the viewpoint of the bank's activities and risks within a country."[33] Yet, when the IMF and creditor governments took the lead in putting together rescue packages for debtors unable to repay their loans, many of the major banks lost much of their ability to decide whether to curtail or increase their loans to certain countries and to determine the terms of these loans.

When the full impact of the debt problem emerged with stark clarity in 1982, in theory, interest rate margins on such loans should have risen to reflect the higher risk associated with the debtor's erosion of creditworthiness, but counterpressure often dictated the opposite result. Not only did the debtor's inability to repay mean that its interest rate margin had to be lowered and interest payments stretched out in order to enable the country to service its debt, but congressional and IMF pressures reinforced perceptions that lower interest rate margins and interest rates were essential in order to ease the debt burden. Of course, a strong argument can be made that it is difficult to figure out a risk premium for a debtor that cannot service its debts, since "no premium can compensate for that."[34]

The banks had little choice but to extend more credit, if necessary, to these countries and reschedule their loans. The alternatives were to declare these countries in default and pursue available assets or to begin the process of writing off the loans as a loss. Such measures held little appeal to the leading money-center banks because they were likely to be detrimental to their well-being or, at a minimum, their earnings. A major cutback—even if a rational move by a single bank—would have had the paradoxical effect, when taken in concert by many major banks, of depriving these developing countries of the required capital to maintain their economic well-being precisely when they needed it most. After rising at an annual rate of about 25 percent during the 1979–1981 period, new credit to Latin American states rose by only 7 percent in 1982 as the "herd instinct" among many commercial banks resulted in an abrupt curtailment in new lending, and voluntary lending has not resumed, and prospects for its resumption are not favorable.[35] To proceed with a default scenario, a bank would, in essence, have to conclude that the likelihood of being repaid is negligible and that it may as well proceed against available assets of the debtor country despite the nasty political disputes likely to ensue. Although private commercial banks are unlikely to be interested in declaring debtor countries in default, they have prepared for such a contingency.[36]

> A loss of market confidence is now a reality. For many countries, particularly in Latin America, important segments of the market for foreign lending have virtually disappeared—in particular, regional bank participation in international loan syndication and private placements intermediated by the investment banks.

Until debt-service uncertainties are resolved, the flow of available credit will be sharply curtailed, and the resolution of those uncertainties in many instances will entail debt reschedulings that will take a significant period of time to prove their workability. We thus have now in place each of the basic elements of classic liquidity squeeze.[37]

Many critics point out that the debt cirsis of 1982 presents a watershed event for international banks and the international financial system. These banks were unwilling to take the "hit" because they could not do so without seriously impairing the value of their outstanding loans, or earnings from these loans, to such countries. In short, rather than absorbing losses, these banks agreed to provide additional funds, even if at a significantly slower rate, to their borrowers. Arguing that taking losses was neither necessary nor appropriate, many banks also acknowledged that they would not be able to absorb losses associated with their outstanding loans to leading debtor countries. Nevertheless, the market was discounting the value of these loans as the stock price of U.S. money-center banks traded below book value.

During the post-1982 era, international banks have extended substantial amounts of new credit to developing countries so that debtors can pay interest. This process, know as "forced" or "involuntary lending," has become a significant new development in sovereign lending. "Forced, or involuntary, lending may be defined as the increase in a bank's exposure to a borrowing nation that is in debt-servicing difficulty and that, because of a loss of creditworthiness, would be unable to attract new lending from banks not already exposed in the country."[38] Government pressures on the banks reportedly included threats by banking regulators to scrutinize the banks' books even closer if they did not generate the loans for certain countries.[39] "Arm-twisting" by governments forcing this process on the banks has been criticized on grounds that: "The banks themselves must decide for which credits they feel they can take responsibility. Neither the IMF nor a central bank can take that decision away from them."[40] Although it is by no means clear that the major banks had a viable alternative to the option of continued lending in reaction to the jolt of 1982, the smaller banks could absorb their limited losses and in many cases have chosen to do so.

Different levels of exposure in debtor countries by U.S. money-center banks, U.S. regional banks, and non-U.S. banks combined with different treatment of reserves and loss provision in the United States and Europe have led to divergent interests among the bankers and threaten the continued viability of the current debt restructuring process. Having the most at risk, U.S. money-center banks used peer pressure on regional U.S. banks and non-U.S. banks to participate in these financial rescue operations. "Recalcitrant banks have had their arms twisted by the IMF, the U.S. Treasury and other official agencies, as well as money center banks. This persuasion has at times been very heavy-handed. Nevertheless, a few of the regional U.S. banks have dragged their feet or even flatly refused to take part."[41]

Even though it is unclear how many of these banks have abandoned "the international lending game," some 20 or 30 banks apparently did not join the Mexico or Brazil 1982–1983 packages, with money-center banks forced to increase their already substantial exposure. Putting in place the 1985 funding packages for Argentina, Ecuador, Costa Rica, and Chile has taken "an unusually long time to syndicate. If in the next few months, a significant number of regional banks drop out, the money centers may have to pick up their shares, and if they do—which is far from certain—the concentration of lending to debt-ridden nations, which is already excessive, will worsen."[42]

In a paradoxical twist, major efforts by many international banks to use country risk analysis to take advantage of the industry's unique diversification opportunities has yielded a high degree of concentration and large exposure in a relatively small number of key developing countries. Many critics have argued that concentration and overexposure are precisely the principles the banks violated because bankers often failed to differentiate—even if, arguably, it was foreseeable—between the debt problems of a few relatively minor debtors and the simultaneous difficulties, including those emanating from systemic risks in the international financial system, of 20 major developing countries in which banks had the highest exposure and highest rate of lending increases.[43]

International banks and regulators tried to analyze individual country risks to identify potential problems and had varying degrees of success. However, they were less successful in coping with systemic risks, since they failed to "anticipate that problems emanating from one or two countries would undermine market confidence and spill over to other countries."[44] The assessment of sovereign lending is a difficult task. Moreover, the effort to gauge a country's debt-service capacity, especially the lack of success in forecasting a country's ability to generate net foreign currency earnings, through a variety of financial ratios to appraise its creditworthiness failed to provide reliable measures of country risk. Indeed, a country's ability to borrow in the private capital markets became a substitute for country risk analysis and reinforced the banks' "herding instincts." The shortcomings of country risk debt-service analysis have implications for the current strategy's effort to restore voluntary lending. Since the strategy relies, in part, on "more debt to solve the debt problem," a marked improvement in the debt-service capacity of the highly indebted developing countries would appear to be a precondition for the reemergence of international banks' enthusiasm for voluntary lending.[45]

Although the debt-servicing difficulties of some countries were prompted, in large part, by systemic factors beyond their immediate control, the high degree of U.S bank exposure and concentration in a few Latin American countries is reflected in Table 3.1. For the major U.S. banks, their Latin American exposure accounts, on average, for about twice their capital. Even as a percentage of their total assets, the Latin American exposure at the end of 1983 was approximately 11 percent for Manufacturers Hanover, 6 percent for Bank of

TABLE 3.1. Latin American Exposure of Top Banking Companies (data as of Dec. 31, 1985; dollars in millions)

Data as of Dec. 31, 1985; (Dollars in Millions)

	Citicorp	Bank-America	Chase Manhattan	Manufact. Hanover	J.P. Morgan	Chemical New York	Security Pacific	Bankers Trust	First Chicago	Wells Fargo	Average Total
Argentina											
Exposure	$1,400	(A)	$920	$1,400	$822	$402	(A)	$383	(A)	$133	$5,077
Nonperforming	$116	(A)	$155	$131	$96	$66.6	(A)	$10	(A)	$32	$596.6
Brazil											
Exposure	$4,700	$2,799	$2,820	$2,200	$1,862	$1,434	$590	$864	$806	$603	$18,678
Nonperforming	$99	$11	$7	$4	$10	$5.7	$13	$30	$8	$15	$202.7
Chile											
Exposure	$500	(A)	(A)	$791	(A)	$369	(A)	(A)	(A)	$104	$1,395
Nonperforming	$13	(A)	(A)	$14	(A)	$4	(A)	(A)	(A)	(A)	$27
Mexico											
Exposure	$2,800	$2,709	$1,680	$1,800	$1,152	$1,471	$520	$1,277	$912	$606	$14,927
Nonperforming	$52	$94	$123	$34	$12	$18	$23	$4	$13	$16	$389
Venezuela											
Exposure	$1,200	$1,450	$1,250	$1,100	(A)	$714	(A)	$419	$425	$259	$5,973
Nonperforming	$295	$405	$200	$16	(A)	$46.9	(A)	$44	$11	$13	$975.9
Reported Exposure	$10,100	$6,958	$6,670	$7,291	$3,836	$4,021	$1,110	$2,141	$1,718	$1,705	$45,550
Reported Nonperforming	$1,575	$510	$485	$199	$118	$137.2	$36	$34	$21	$76	$2,191
Exposure as % of Equity	130%	153%	175%	205%	87%	143%	45%	85%	82%	117%	122.1%
Stockholders' Equity	$7,765	$4,547	$3,795	$3,547	$4,392	$2,820	$2,439	$2,495	$2,090	$1,458	$

(A) The exposure to this country generally is less than 1% of total loans and other investments and is therefore not broken out in exact figures. In some cases, such as for Chile, banks have provided figures for comparative purposes, although the exposure is below the level required for full disclosure.

Source: Gordon Matthews, "Big Banks' Latin American Exposure Decline Noticeably But Remain Large," *The American Banker*, March 31, 1986, p. 9. Reprinted with permission.

America, and in the 7 to 9 percent range for such major banks as Crocker National, Chase Manhattan, Citicorp, Irving Bank, Chemical, and Marine Midland. Consequently, international banks have found themselves "locked in," even if their preference was to pull back from their international lending activities.

Yet since 1982, international banks' net new lending to Latin debtor countries has dropped sharply, thereby reducing the relative exposure of U.S. banks to debtors in the region (see Table 3.1). These major commercial banks have improved their capital position as they expanded in other areas while halting their outstanding international exposure. In addition, the percentage of nonperforming loans has dropped from 7 percent in 1983 to 4 percent in 1985, with most of these loans outstanding to private borrowers, not governments. Nonetheless, the international exposure of major commercial banks remains high and insures their continuing stake in a successful resolution of the debt crisis.[46]

Some bankers and banking consultants have continued to insist that the large external debt of some key developing countries held by private banks is no reason for alarm. This school of thought rejects the argument that a large debt makes a country less creditworthy and advocates continued use of professional country risk evaluation to diversify a bank's portfolio on a country-by-country basis.[47] However, the country-by-country approach, the essence of country risk analysis, may have left many banks vulnerable to the impact of global or systemic factors on their borrowers. Although some country risk analysts were cognizant of the possibility of such global occurrences, they discounted its significance.

The repayment problems of major debtors have caused and are expected to continue to pose a real earnings burden on money-center U.S. banks whose performance will suffer. Moody's, the credit rating agency, has downgraded these banks because they have failed to provide a realistic value for their exposure to developing countries. In June 1985, Moody's announced that it was reviewing about $7.2 billion in Manufacturers Hanover securities because the bank's over $1 billion exposure in Argentina "will depress profitability further and limit capital adequacy to levels which may be inconsistent with current ratings."[48] Moody's has estimated that if these banks had treated their problem loans as nonperforming and recognized service payments only when received, their earnings for 1983 would have ranged from 26 percent lower for J.P. Morgan to 60 percent lower for Manufacturers Hanover. Despite its assessment that foreign loan risks and turmoil in domestic and international markets may precipitate a crisis in some U.S. banks, Moody's concludes that the U.S. government will not allow major U.S. banks to fail because they are "too important to the economy, too interconnected and too confidence sensitive—and the LDC loan problems too pervasive of the international banking system."[49] Indeed, some U.S. bank regulators have testified that the U.S. government will not allow the leading U.S. banks to fail, as demonstrated by the actions taken when Continental Illinois ran into severe problems.

Many bankers involved in lending additional funds to Mexico and Argentina in 1984 were reportedly irate at the alleged interference by the Federal Reserve, the IMF, and the Treasury Department in attempting to reduce the interest rate margins on those loans by encouraging these governments to demand lower rates from their creditor U.S. banks.[50] During 1984 the IMF and others were urging banks to reward countries that were implementing IMF adjustment programs by reducing interest rate spreads and providing them with multi-year reschedulings, as was done for Mexico. Ironically, however, interest rates were rising in mid-1984 as major efforts were being made to reduce the interest rate margins, thereby negating much of the effort to reduce the debtor countries' debt burden and prompting sharp attacks from leading Latin American leaders. Furthermore, bankers' skepticism about Argentina's ability to comply with its IMF agreement and the terms of its 1984 loans appeared to undercut the argument that debtor countries were being rewarded for their cooperation.

> Argentina, with a rescheduling package almost identical to Mexico's and an interest rate only one-quarter of a percentage point higher, is reaping rewards for intransigence that are almost equal to the rewards for Mexican cooperation. The low cost of noncooperation has weakened Argentina's incentive to comply with any agreement, while permitting that country to make disastrous policy changes.[51]

Yet Argentina did make a dramatic turnaround. Furthermore, by 1986 a sharp reduction in real interest rates and a substantial fall in the value of the dollar were providing many debtor countries with some debt relief. However, oil-exporting countries, particularly Mexico, saw these benefits offset by the substantial decline in the price of oil.

ROLE OF THE IMF

As a means of providing the necessary flexibility and insuring that unique circumstances could be adequately addressed, the U.S. government's debt strategy placed a premium on country-by-country rescue packages and economic adjustment programs to be negotiated between debtor countries and the IMF. The United States supported the IMF's leading role in bringing discipline both to international lending and key debtor countries' economies. The Reagan administration's request for increased IMF resources elicited criticism from those who charged that the IMF was bailing out the banks or acting on their behalf such that they would not be required to absorb losses.

The IMF as well as other official creditors may have to provide increased resources to debtor countries as the pace of commercial bank international lending decreases in response to perceived risks associated with large exposure and high degrees of concentration. The debt problem has been accompanied by the transformation of the roles of the participating parties. Commercial bankers, chastised by the results of go-go international banking, have been forced to become reluctant creditors to countries that once were their darlings. Formerly aloof central bankers have become peddlers of international financial rescue packages to lenders and borrowers. Meanwhile, the IMF has sought to counter the effort of many banks to withdraw by keeping them involved in extending new loans.

Although its resources in relation to the overall debt burden are limited, the IMF has evolved as an institution and taken the lead in putting together financing packages and providing countries with a stamp of approval for commercial bank lending. Some have disparaged the IMF's role with respect to the factors involved in the current international debt crisis as doing little more than standing on the sidelines and shouting encouragement.[52] Although this characterization is more charitable than former U.S. Secretary of the Treasury Connally's reported observation that the IMF is "a museum where everything that isn't stuffed ought to be,"[53] the IMF's current role has changed substantially since its days as a custodian of a system of pegged exchange rates. That system provided a set of rules for countries to maintain the exchange rates of their currencies and provided a signal for the need for countries to undertake domestic adjustments. However, strains on the international monetary system caused the breakdown of the pegged exchange rate system in 1971 and its replacement with a floating exchange rate system.

The IMF's role of aiding countries in their adjustment process has led to its active involvement in the international debt problem. Although its establishment was, in part, stimulated by the debt problems of the 1920s and 1930s, the IMF's efforts in grappling with external debt issues has been a recent development. Not only did the IMF assist in formulating adjustment programs and additional financing for key debtor countries, but in a number of cases it led the way in putting together "funding packages." By making the extension of its resources contingent on increased participation by the commercial banks, the IMF helped provide some discipline to the extension of such bank credits when time was of the essence. Furthermore, agreement to increase the IMF's resources and enlarge the General Arrangements to Borrow served not only to buttress the IMF's capability to continue its role in the debt problem, but also served as a symbolic signal of the international community's determination to preserve the stability of the global financial system.[54]

The IMF has exercised its leverage in its dealings with the banks as well as in its negotiations with debtor countries. The IMF's actions with respect to the banks has been justified on the basis that "the prodding of commercial banks by the IMF is to be interpreted more as an indication of the conditions necessary for the financial viability of adjustment programmes than as undue interference with the banks' independence in their decision-making."[55] Nonetheless, the major commercial banks agreed to participate in these IMF-sponsored arrangements primarily because it was to their benefit to do so. Since the option of a cessation of future lending was not viable in light of the negative impact of such an action of the banks, the money-center banks had little choice but to agree to the IMF's game plan, which involved providing funds to as well as enforcing adjustment programs by the debtor countries.

The IMF—and its managing director, Jacques de Larosiere—has been credited with playing the catalyst in putting together rescue operations in the form of funding packages that have kept the financial squeeze in Mexico, Brazil, Argentina, and other countries from turning into a full-fledged crisis for the international monetary system. The IMF has been involved in a series of tough negotiations with several of the key developing countries over their adjustment programs. The IMF also made it clear to commercial banks, especially those with large exposure in such leading debtor countries as Mexico and Brazil, that they would have to extend billions of dollars in new loans to these countries prior to the IMF's having in place an adjustment program with these countries. In some cases agreement on a letter of intent between the IMF and the debtor countries served as the basis for extension of commercial loans. Not only was this a fundamental change for the commercial banks that had become accustomed to waiting until an IMF program was in effect before considering whether to extend new loans, but the IMF also forced the commercial banks to put up additional new money as part of new IMF programs.

The IMF has been transformed from John Connally's museum or, as others have characterized it, "a creature of rhetoric, issuing toothless encyclicals on world inflation, trade and currency stability," to an institution willing to play the "role of economic disciplinarian and watchdog" for the adjustment process debtor developing countries are undergoing to bring their debt problems under control.[56] In an effort to retain their creditworthiness and restore their economies, many key debtor countries have concluded that they have little choice but to agree to the IMF's prescription for their ills. Self-doubt about their country risk capabilities led commercial banks to transfer this role to the IMF by conditioning additional lending on a debtor country's compliance with an IMF program.

Critics of the IMF's newly discovered active role have questioned whether it has the tools necessary to fulfill it. "They question the wisdom of the often Draconian restraints the IMF prescribes. They wonder about LDC governments' ability to sell those restraints to their people. And they worry about the social powderkeg that the fund risks setting off with its programs—however beneficial they may be for LDC's in the long run."[57]

Some major banks have also begun to have second thoughts about the IMF's power and their granting of new loans, although these banks have had little choice but to agree to provide such additional loans. This process has allowed the IMF to direct these banks to lend more money as part of financing arrangements— "bailing the banks in" deeper, as Secretary Regan has phrased it. "The International Monetary Fund, through its Managing Director, has already made history by virtually requiring the banks to commit new funds to Argentina, Brazil, and Mexico as a condition for its own lending."[58]

As one investment banker has noted, "the fund was in a position analogous to the last lender to a company on the verge of bankruptcy. It was really the only party initially bringing new money to the table. And that meant that it could not only make demands on the debtors, which it had always done, but it could make demands on the *creditors*, too."[59] The leading banks' high key debtor country concentration, significant exposure, and inability to absorb losses from these loans without a major impact on the banks' earnings motivated them to agree to the IMF's terms.

The IMF was troubled by the implications arising from the sharp cutbacks in commercial bank lending. The debt service payments of the major borrowers exceeded their new borrowing by $7 billion in 1982 and $21 billion in 1983. In short, the rate of increase in international lending was reduced significantly and the major debtor countries became net capital exporters.[60] The continuing decline in net new lending available to the debtor countries as a means of stimulating growth was one of the major factors behind the Baker Plan of October 1985.

Some argue that for the commercial banks to remain in the developing country lending game, they need to be sure that the IMF has sufficient resources to maintain the effectiveness of its conditionality tool. That is, the IMF provides the banks with an assurance that the financial package being put together will be enforced. The debtor country, as a condition for receiving additional funds, is required to adopt "sound adjustment policies," that is, get its economic house in order by adopting belt-tightening measures.[61] The IMF has been sensitive to the charge that implementation of its principle of conditionality on the current $30 billion in credits it has outstanding to developing countries causes undue austerity, stimulates cuts in the growth rate of developing countries, reduces their imports from creditor developed countries, and generates social and political repercussions. Yet the IMF's ability to "bail in" the banks is based not only on its ability to provide additional resources and enforce its conditionality but also on the "good housekeeping seal" provided by a country's acceptance of an IMF adjustment program.

The IMF's conditions for use of its resources can involve agreement or "conditionality" on numerous economic policies including fiscal, monetary, exchange rate, external debt management, and foreign investment. Its certification of a country's economic performance has become one of its most important functions from the perspective of the international banking community. As a multilateral financial institution, the IMF can often insist on conditions for a country to implement that might be untenable for a private bank to urge on a borrower and act as the catalyst for additional commercial lending. These austerity measures have come under criticism from many quarters, including a senior Brazilian official who framed the issue as follows: "If the IMF's prescription of austerity and slower economic growth to get a country back on its feet is applied to one or two countries, the medicine can work. But if it is given to an entire continent—or, worse to every developing country in the world—then we all die from the cure."[62]

Harsh critics, such as Allen Meltzer of Carnegie-Mellon University, have indicted the IMF on several grounds. In particular, they argue that the IMF is the

perpetrator of an international Ponzi scheme whereby U.S. banks keep bad loans on their books at face value, lend more money so that their debtors can meet interest payments, rely on the IMF's injecting funds into debtors to assist the process, and paradoxically end up showing increased earnings despite the deteriorating quality of their loan portfolios. Indeed, the critics maintain that by encouraging the banks' belief in ultimate bailout, the IMF inspired reckless loan policies in the first place.[63]

The IMF has come under criticism for not developing initiatives for international monetary reform. It has also been attacked for denying the very existence of a global debt crisis and treating the debt issue as a series of case-by-case problems to be tackled as ad hoc and unique country adjustment programs.[64] Yet the IMF has been credited with putting in place the financial packages that have attained the critical element of time. In short, it has provided the international financial system with several crucial benefits, including guiding the overall debt process, advising and helping countries design effective adjustment and financing programs, and coordinating aspects of complex international financial arrangements, including encouragement of commercial banks' willingness to negotiate multi-year rescheduling arrangements for countries that have made progress in their economic adjustment efforts. By obtaining time to prepare against the onslaught of the debt crunch, the IMF is viewed as having defused a potential crisis by focusing on the short term, while aware that "the longer-term problems of LDC debt can only be solved by an expansion of world trade, lower interest rates, far greater concessional aid (especially through the World Bank), and a sustained Western recovery."[65]

RESCHEDULING

Restructuring of sovereign debt has become a commonplace feature of recent international banking activities and reflects the severity of the global debt problem. Rescheduling may involve a restructuring, that is, changes in contractual terms such as lengthening maturities or financing. In essence, rescheduling is the extension of new credit to substitute for outstanding debt. Banks prefer to refinance because they can continue to treat the claim as a "performing loan."

Not only is a rescheduling an admission by both the lender and borrower that the loan cannot be paid on time, but many of the reschedulings for key debtor countries have included a significant infusion of new capital. Typically, a rescheduled bank loan requires the debtor country to continue to make its interest payments on the full amount of outstanding debt but over an extended period of time.

There has been a dramatic rise in the frequency and magnitude of these reschedulings during the recent past, climbing from about $5 billion in 1980 to over $100 billion in 1986. Since the August 1982 Mexican financial crisis, the total amount of rescheduled external debt owed international banks by 15 debtor countries has exceeded $100 billion, over one-half of their outstanding debt.[66] During 1983 five sovereign borrowers—Mexico, Brazil, Argentina, Venezuela, and Poland—were in the midst of rescheduling approximately $75 billion and 24 developing countries rescheduled $67 billion of foreign debt, with about $56 billion owed to commercial banks.[67] In late 1982 and early 1983, Mexico and Brazil restructured massive amounts of debt owed to international banks—$35 billion for Mexico and about $5 billion for Brazil. Most of that renegotiated amount was for public sector debt and principal due in 1983–1984, which was stretched out for six to eight years. By 1985, Mexico and Brazil were seeking 15-year rescheduling of about $100 billion owed to commercial banks during the mid-1980s. By 1986, Mexico, Brazil, and Venezuela alone had rescheduled loans in excess of $100 billion with the banks providing improved terms even when the debtor country had not agreed to implement an IMF economic adjustment program.

Before the emergence of the post-1982 debt problem, reschedulings were by and large confined to debts owed by developing countries to creditor governments or to private lenders with a creditor-government guarantee. These reschedulings were negotiated through the Paris Club, a debt-rescheduling process organized from the vantage point of the official creditors.[68] Reschedulings of significant amounts of debt owed to international banks were relatively rare, although two noteworthy exceptions were the rescheduling of Turkey's $3 billion external debt in 1979 and Poland's $4.8 billion in 1982.[69] While the Paris Club has evolved some rules and procedures for dealing with creditor government loans to debtor governments, most bankers believe that they cannot develop a systematic approach for restructuring international debts owed to the banking system. Nonetheless, an advisory group mechanism has developed as bank exposure has grown. The restructuring of sovereign debt to banks is done by an advisory or steering group usually led by the banks having the largest exposure in the country and the ones that took the lead in the syndicated loans. Initially the regional or smaller banks were willing to follow the lead of the large banks when they entered this market but have recently begun to feel that their interests are not adequately considered or protected during the restructuring.

The degree of confidence a country generates among its bank creditors, as well as the prudent policies it is willing to follow, is an important consideration when private banks are faced by the need to reschedule debts. "The rescheduling of debt due to private banks will seriously damage a country's creditworthiness with private lenders, and will therefore impair future access to needed private capital."[70] However, a bank creditor may have little choice but to reschedule its loans to borrowing countries, especially if such loans constitute a large percentage of its assets and a cessation of interest payments would have substantial repercussions for the bank.

The steps taken by Mexico and Brazil in 1982 to reschedule their debts provide two distinct models. The Mexicans presented the international banking community with a sudden, dramatic case and demanded immediate action. Mexico's financing rescue package provided by the United States was arranged with minimal publicity over a weekend. In seeking to reassure the international banking community, the Brazilians had difficulty putting together a viable financing package and their creditworthiness suffered during the intervening months. "The essence of the Mexican approach was an instant moratorium, the simultaneous appointment of a single advisory committee to represent all creditor banks, the prompt arrangement of bridging finance, a delayed imposition of exchange controls, but one which was not delayed excessively, prompt action to maintain interbank lines, and clear proposals at each stage for the amounts and terms of the debt being restructured."[71]

However well-intentioned the Brazilian effort to allay the fears of the international banks by suggesting that their case was different from Mexico's, Brazil did not succeed in insulating itself from bankers' reactions toward Latin America because of the Mexican aftershock. "On the contrary, by hesitating to act more promptly and decisively, the Brazilian authorities allowed the external debt situation to worsen and, justifiably or otherwise, conveyed the impression of indecisiveness to the foreign creditor banks which they were seeking to reassure."[72]

Between 1978 and 1980, principal for most borrowing countries was restructured such that the maturity was stretched to five or six years, a two-year grace period during which no payments were due, and lending margins were set at 1.25 to 1.5 percent over LIBOR. Until 1980, Brazil had obtained lending margins under 1 percent, while Mexico had obtained 0.5 percent only two months prior to its August 1982 financial crisis. However, the 1982 restructuring for Mexico and Brazil included eight-year stretch-outs, a two-year grace period, with lending margins well over 2 percent and substantial arrangement fees. By 1984 negotiations were being conducted to achieve even longer terms, such as ten-year stretch-outs and five-year grace periods, and lower margins, while the 1985 Mexican rescheduling is for a 15-year term. During the first half of 1986 U.S. interest rates declined dramatically and the international banks agreed to reschedule $31 billion of Brazil's debt with interest rates spread over LIBOR reduced from 2.25 percent to 1.125 percent. These interest rates concessions were, in part, granted by the banks in response to demands by the debtor countries.

In essence, at the initial phase of the debt crisis, creditor banks sought belated compensation for the favorable terms they had provided in the borrowers' market that characterized most of the 1970s and the early 1980s. If arrangement fees are taken into account, the first wave of post-1982 debt restructurings yielded banks about 2 percent a year more than the terms on which most of that debt was originally contracted.[73] Of course, these yields are only realized if the debt is in fact paid, and many of the 1984 negotiations were aimed at easing the terms of repayment, in part, by reducing these spreads and rescheduling fees.

Banks have had to include short-terms debts, that is, those loans originally made for a period less than one year, as well as interest arrears in their long-term restructuring of borrowing countries' debts. Initially they also resisted pressures aimed at restoring interbank lines, that is, deposits by banks in each other, to banks in certain debtor countries and maintaining full trade-financing arrangements for such countries.

The *Allied* case raised the issue whether a foreign government, in this case Costa Rica, could unilaterally impose exchange controls such that its private foreign debt obligations could not be paid and the loan agreement would be unenforceable in U.S. courts. Although the case raised the issues of sovereign immunity and act of state doctrine, the U.S. Court of Appeals for the Second Circuit initially ruled that the principle of comity required it to allow a foreign government to do so because U.S. policy supported Costa Rica's action, but it reversed itself after rehearing the case. The U.S. government was not only concerned that the initial decision could encourage other debtor countries to cease servicing their foreign debt obligations, but that the commercial banks would be deterred from providing additional loans if they could not enforce them in U.S. courts. The court emphasized that by assuming that the U.S. government's policy favored private debt rescheduling regardless of this unilateral cutoff of a creditor's rights, it had misconstrued the U.S. government's policy regarding the management of the debt crisis. The court agreed that a foreign government's unilateral repudiation of its loan obligation would not be consistent with the goal of an orderly resolution of the international debt problem.[74]

Although many commercial bankers argue that despite the contingency planning they have done to cope with defaults, they are not concerned about formal defaults on the part of debtor countries, there has been increased worry about "default by attrition" or creeping default.[75] One debtor country has had its debts—including principal and interest arrears—restructured on a regular basis. Since the country fails to meet the terms and renegotiates every time, it is widely recognized that this case, indeed, possesses all the attributes of a default in all but name. This is so since formally the creditor is required to declare the debtor in default as the first step in a process to move against the debtor's assets in satisfaction of the claim. Many banks are hesitant to take these measures because they would then be forced into writing off loans to such a country, a step that would not be especially significant with respect to countries with relatively small debts, but would have enormous consequences in the case of large debtor countries.

By 1986, commercial banks have come under increasing criticism for treating the debt crisis as a short-term bank earnings, balance sheet, and income statement issue rather than trying to adopt a long-term solution. Furthermore, "the politics are turning adverse" because those in power in Latin America cannot "stay in power without concessions" as the perception sinks in that the reason for their austerity is to avoid the impairment of the stock price of "gringo banks."[76] Many bankers have expressed grave doubts about the ability to restore normal market credit conditions for the debtor countries. In his February 22, 1986 speech, Mexico's President De La Madrid argued that Mexico had done its share by adjusting. Arguing that the international community would have to share in the search for a viable solution from the perspective of Mexico's vital interests, he put the international banks on notice that they too must bear part of the cost by declaring that "it now behooves our creditors to make, at the least, an effort equivalent to the great task and sacrifice which the Mexican people have endured." [77]

Yet, while international commercial bankers have sought to protect their existing loan exposure and the income they generate, the economies of the lending debtor countries have not grown enough to relieve the political pressure of the debt burden. The slowdown in commercial bank lending to the debtor countries may be a rational reaction to their large exposure, but may undercut an "implicit bargain" made between the banks and the debtors, namely, that adjustments by the debtors would result in the resumption of increased lending by the commercial banks. Whether the commercial banks will be willing voluntarily to increase their exposure or reduce the debt service burden in order to stimulate growth in the debtor countries remains a major uncertainty in the unfolding of the debt crisis and undercuts confidence regarding its successful resolution.[78]

A key ingredient of the Baker Plan is its call on commercial banks to support structural adjustment to achieve growth in debtor countries by providing them with net new lending. The U.S. government views such lending as in their self-interest since

> the banks can only gain from providing additional financing which improves the creditworthiness of their existing clients. The banks know that without growth in the debtor nations—and an improved ability to earn foreign exchange—they cannot expect to be repaid, nor, to put it bluntly, can they expect to continue favorable earnings on assets of declining quality. The banks also know that growth must be financed in large part from private capital resources.[79]

Although international commercial banks as well as the IMF and World Bank have endorsed the Baker Plan, it has encountered substantial skepticism and movement has been slow. The commercial banks have welcomed "Baker's initiative as a positive and constructive development'' and confirmed ''their willingness to play their part on a case-by-case basis, provided that all other parties, governmental, institutional, and banking, do the same.''[80]

Commercial banks stepped into a new role as they became increasingly involved in balance-of-payments financing. However, their lack of adequate information and increasing exposure threatened the integrity of the international banking system, prompting bank regulatory agencies in creditor countries to reevaluate and redouble their efforts.

Many commercial bankers have concluded that several key assumptions underlying their expectations of bank lending were incorrect and have yielded a high debt-servicing burden for their borrowers, with accompanying unpleasant consquences. Some bankers view any additional lending as simply pouring in good money after bad and have little hope for ever being repaid. They consider such lending to be in violation of a cardinal rule, namely, not lending to provide funds for debt service. Some observers argue that this is a practice that has come to be sanctioned by bank regulators because of the circumstances confronting the parties as efforts are made to provide the participants with additional time to improve the situation.

NOTES

1. Michael Edgerton, "Western Banks, Poor Nations Costar in Drama of Global Debt," *Chicago Tribune,* June 10, 1983.

2. Richard P. Cooley, chairman of Seattle-First National Bank, as quoted in *Business Week,* "Behind the Banking Turmoil," October 29, 1984, p. 101.

3. Alex E. Fleming,"International Lending Is Now Likely to Slow After Its Recent Period of Substantial Growth," *IMF Survey,* October 4, 1982, p. 331.

4. Irving S. Friedman, *The World Debt Dilemma: Managing Country Risk* (Washington, D.C. and Philadelphia: Council for International Banking Studies and Robert Morris Associates, 1983), p. 18.

5. Anthony Sampson, *The Money Lenders* (New York: Viking Press, 1981).

6. David C. Mulford, "The U.S. Debt Initiative: Toward Stronger Growth in the Debtor Nations," before the Orion Royal Bank Conference, The Plaisteres Hall, London, England, February 4, 1986.

7. T.H. Donaldson, *Lending in International Commercial Banking* (Surrey, England: Macmillan, 1979), p. 68.

8. Bahram Nowzard, Richard C. Williams, et al., *External Indebtedness of Developing Countries*, Occasional Paper No. 3, Washington, D.C.: IMF, May 1981, p. 6.

9. Penelope Hartland-Thunberg, "Vulnerabilities of the International Financial Mechanism," in Thibault de Saint Phalle (ed.), *The International Financial Crisis: An Opportunity for Constructive Action* (Washington, D.C.: Center for Strategic and International Studies, 1983), p. 5.

10. Rimmer de Vries, "Perspective: Country Risk, A Banker's View," in Richard J. Herring (ed.), *Managing International Risk* (Cambridge: Cambridge University Press, 1983).

11. Irving S. Friedman, *The Emerging Role of Private Banks in the Developing World* (New York: Citicorp, 1977), p. 32.

12. See, for example, ibid.; Paul M. Watson, *Debt and the Developing Countries: New Problems and New Actors* (Washington, D.C.: Overseas Development Council, 1978); Lawrence G. Franko and Marilyn J. Seiber (eds.), *Developing Country Debt* (New York: Pergamon Press, 1979).

13. Friedman, *The Emerging Role.*

14. Ibid., p. 33.

15. Sampson, op. cit.; George C. Abbott, *International Indebtedness and the Developing Countries* (London: Croom Helm, 1979).

16. Friedman, *The Emerging Role*.

17. Watson, op. cit., p. 49.

18. Friedman, *The Emerging Role*, p. 67.

19. Ibid., p. 55.

20. Watson, op cit., pp. 22 and 58.

21. Peter Field, "Meet the New Breed of Banker: The Political Risk Expert," *Euromoney*, July 1980, p. 15; Pancras Nagy, *Country Risk* (London: Euromoney Publications, 1979), p. 13.

22. Nagy, op. cit., p. 14.

23. Lynn D. Feintech, "Political Risk Assessment at Bank of America," in Theodore H. Moran (ed.), *International Political Risk Assessment* (Washington, D.C.: Georgetown University, 1980), p. 74.

24. *Institutional Investor*, "Rating Country Risk," September 1979 and "The Credit Rating Shake-Up," September 1980; *Euromoney*, "The Country Risk League Table," October 1979.

25. J.N. Robinson, "Is It Possible to Assess Country Risk?" *The Banker*, January 1981.

26. Field, op. cit., p. 15.

27. Ibid., p. 15.

28. Louis Kraar, "The Multinationals Get Smarter About Political Risks," *Fortune*, March 24, 1980.

29. Field, op. cit., p. 19.

30. Helen Hughes, "Prospective: The Risks of Lending to Developing Countries," in Richard J. Herring (ed.), *Managing International Risk* (Cambridge: Cambridge University Press, 1983), p. 168.

31. Friedman, *The Emerging Role*, p. 66.

32. Ibid., p. 48.

33. Ibid., p. 49.

34. Pedro-Pablo Kuczynski, "Latin American Debt: Act Two," *Foreign Affairs*, Fall 1983, p. 25.

35. Takeshi Watanabe, Jacques Lesourne, and Robert S. McNamara, *Facilitating Development in A Changing Third World* (New York: The Trilateral Commission, 1983), p. 46.

36. Linda Sandler, "US Banks Prepare for Possibility of Third World Debt Repudiation," *The Wall Street Journal*, July 6, 1984.

37. William S. Ogden, "The Nature of the LDC Debt Problem," remarks at the Manhattan Institute of Policy Research, October 1982, as quoted in Watanabe et al., op. cit., p. 46.

38. William R. Cline, *International Debt and the Stability of the World Economy* (Washington, D.C.: Institute for International Economics, 1983); William R. Cline, *International Debt* (Washington, D.C., Institute for International Economics, 1984).

39. Benjamin Cohen, "International Debt and Linkage Strategies: Some Foreign-Policy Implications for the United States," *International Organization*, Autumn 1985.

40. Karl Otto Pohl (Bundesbank president) as quoted in Linda Sandler, "Is Discounting Sovereign Debt the Way Out? " *Institutional Investor*, July 1983, p. 73.

41. Christine A. Bogdanowicz-Bindert, "Small Debtors: The Smouldering Crisis and U.S. Interest in an Orderly Solution," House Subcommittee on International Development Institutions and Finance, June 27, 1985.

42. Ibid.

43. De Vries, op. cit.

44. Comments by Nicholas Sargen in Jack M. Guttentag and Richard J. Herring, *The Current Crisis in International Lending* (Washington, D.C.: The Brookings Institution, 1985), p. 36.

45. Jesus Silva-Herzog, "The Evolution and Prospects of the Latin American Debt Problem," paper presented at conference "Beyond the Debt Crisis," London, January 27–28, 1986. See also Sargen in Guttentag and Herring, op. cit.

46. Gordon Matthews, "Big Banks' Latin American Exposures Decline Noticeably but Remain Large," *The American Banker*, March 25, 1986.

47. Friedman, *The World Debt*.

48. Donald Shoultz, "Monetary Fund Leader Backing Argentina Plan," *The American Banker*, June 12, 1985.

49. As quoted in *The Financial Times*, "Problem Loans Cut Real Profits of Main U.S. Banks," September 25, 1984.

50. *Business Week*, "Third World Debt: It's the Fed vs. the Bankers," January 9, 1984, p. 47.

51. Paul Craig Roberts, "Argentina Sold the IMF a Prescription for Disaster," *Business Week*, December 24, 1984, p. 12.

52. M.S. Mendelsohn, "Fireman's Ball in Washington." *The Banker*, September 1983, p. 25.

53. Lenny Glynn, "A Jacques de Larosiere Report Card," *Institutional Investor*, September 1983, p. 123.

54. Lamberto Dini, "Where the International Financial System Needs Strengthening," *The Banker*, September 1983, p. 29.

55. Ibid., p. 34.

56. *Institutional Investor*, "Is the IMF Too Tough?," September 1983.

57. Ibid.

58. Watanabe et al., op. cit., p. 51.

59. Richard Weinart as quoted in Glynn, op. cit., p. 123.

60. *Debt and the Developing World* (Washington, D.C.: The World Bank, 1984).

61. Hobart Rowen, "The Washington Agenda," *Institutional Investor*, September 1983, p. 188.

62. Brazilian Industry Minister João Camilo Penna as quoted in *Time*, "Third World Lightning Rod," July 2, 1984, p. 49.

63. Peter Brimelow, "Why the U.S. Shouldn't Fill the IMF's Till," *Fortune*, November 14, 1983.

64. Glynn, op. cit., p. 126.

65. Ibid.

66. M.S. Mendelsohn, *Commercial Banks and the Restructuring of Cross-Border Debt* (New York: Group of Thirty, 1983), p. 3. See also *Development and Debt Service* (Washington, D.C.: The World Bank, 1986).

67. *Debt and the Developing World*, p. viii.

68. Alexis Rieffel, "The Paris Club, 1978–1983," *Columbia Journal of Transnational Law*, Vol. 23, No. 1, 1984.

69. Mendelsohn, *Commercial Banks*, p. 3.

70. Friedman, *The Emerging Role*, p. 69.

71. Mendelsohn, *Commercial Banks*, p. 21.

72. Ibid., p. 23.

73. Ibid., p. 8, and for data on widening spreads since 1982, see *Debt and the Developing World*.

74. See also Barry C. Barnett, Sergio J. Galvis, and Ghislain Gouraige, Jr., "On Third World Debt," *Harvard International Law Journal*, Winter 1984.

75. Sandler, op. cit.

76. David C. Cates as quoted in Burt Solomon, "Feeling the Pain," *National Journal*, March 29, 1986, p. 772.

77. *Foreign Broadcast Information Service*, "Mexico: De La Madrid Speech on Economic Situation," February 22, 1986.

78. Karin Lissakers, testimony before the Joint Economic Committee, June 24, 1985.

79. Mulford, op. cit., p. 5.

80. *Morgan Guaranty Trust Company*, Press Release, December 11, 1985.

4

The Role of The
Bank Regulators

A simultaneous default by Mexico and Brazil in 1982 would have wiped out the capital of the top nine U.S. banks. U.S. bank regulators have been faulted for not having taken appropriate steps to prevent the dramatic increase in international lending by U.S. banks that placed them in such a vulnerable position. They have also been sharply criticized for allowing major U.S. banks to create the financial illusion of generating income they do not have.[1] The importance and vulnerability of these leading U.S. banks were reflected in the assurance by some U.S. bank regulators that they would not allow the top 11 U.S. banks to fail.[2]

Although the U.S. regulatory framework treats domestic and international banking operation in similar fashion, the 1982 debt crisis triggered pressures for greater regulations of international banking at a time when a series of domestic deregulation initiatives was underway. U.S. bank regulators were in a peculiar position. They were keenly aware that an abrupt cessation or curtailment of such lending could lead to the financial collapse of some key debtor countries as well as major U.S. banks and possibly of the international banking system. Accordingly, they sought to avert the "herd instinct" of many banks whose initial reaction was to try to curb their international loan exposure.[3] Although the value of these loans was considered to be less than that reflected by the banks' books, bank regulators and accountants stretched "the limits of generally accepted accounting practices in order to keep LDC debts off the lists of nonperforming loans."[4] Although this tactic served to maintain continued bank lending by not significantly harming bank earnings, it did depress the stock of the money center banks as the market discounted the value of these international loans.[5] Under pressure from Congress, U.S. regulators also suggested tighter regulatory controls on future activities of major U.S. banks to avoid a recurrence of the situation and relieve the vulnerability of leading U.S. banks.

57

Banks in the United States and abroad are subject to a variety of regulations designed to ensure the safety and soundness of the banking system and their conformity to laws and regulations. While each country has its own regulatory framework, the rise of global banking during the 1970s has fostered the development of voluntary cooperative arrangements among supervisory authorities in many countries. Despite numerous variations, most countries have adopted more formal regulatory frameworks and have devoted considerable attention to such prudential considerations as capital adequacy requirements, country risk exposure, and principles of parental responsibilities of foreign branches.[6] We will examine the role of U.S. bank supervisors in dealing with the debt crisis by focusing on the following issues: (1) the purpose and functions of bank regulation; (2) the process of banking supervision as an important foundation for understanding the supervision of international banking activities; (3) how U.S. bank regulators oversee the international activities of U.S. banks; and (4) the efforts of banking authorities in various countries to develop multilateral cooperation.

U.S. BANK SUPERVISION AND REGULATION

The United States operates a dual banking system that provides for both state and federal chartering of banks, recognizes the rights of individual states to determine many of the banking laws within their boundaries, and prevents banks from branching across state lines. Former Chairman of the Board of Governors of the Federal Reserve System, Arthur Burns, has noted that the U.S. regulatory structure is exceedingly complex. He described it as a system of ''parallel and sometimes overlapping regulatory powers, a jurisdictional maze that boggles the mind.'' He was referring to the many state and federal agencies that regulate the approximately 41,000 depository institutions in the United States. In part, this overlapping, jurisdictional maze reflects unique historical and political factors as well as the diversity of U.S. financial institutions. The fragmentation of the U.S. financial services industry is rooted in laws passed during the 1930s in response to the public perception that many of the financial problems leading to the Depression were caused by conflicts of interest. There are many legislative restrictions and limitations placed on banks, including the types of business they can engage in, their geographic expansion, loan limits to a single borrower, the types of investments they can make, restrictions on merger and acquisition activity, and rules on how much capital is required to operate.

Certain federal regulatory agencies—including the Securities and Exchange Commission for securities regulation, the Department of Justice for enforcement of antitrust and criminal laws, and the Department of Labor for employment practices—have some jurisdiction over depository institutions. The Office of the Comptroller of the Currency (OCC), part of the U.S. Treasury, is the chartering and supervising agency for national banks, which are automatically entitled to Federal Deposit Insurance Corporation (FDIC) coverage and are required by law to be members of the Federal Reserve System. State-chartered banks that become members of the Federal Reserve System (FRS), are also entitled to FDIC insurance. They are supervised at the state level by authorities of the chartering state and at the federal level by the Federal Reserve. State-chartered banks that do not join the FRS must be approved by the FDIC if they are to obtain deposit insurance and are supervised by state authorities and, at the federal level, by the FDIC.

As the central bank of the United States, the FRS, an independent agency, combines its bank supervisory and regulatory activities, including those of all bank holding companies and their nonbank subsidiaries, with its basic responsibilities for implementing monetary policy. The FDIC is also an independent agency of the federal government whose primary task is to provide deposit insurance for commercial banks. In an effort to improve coordination among the various federal financial regulatory agencies, in 1979 Congress created the Federal Financial Institutions Examination Council (FFIEC).

In the United States, supervision and regulation of banks serve many, sometimes overlapping or conflicting goals, including: (1) maintenance of economic stability; (2) maintenance of a financially sound banking system; (3) minimization of bank failures; (4) avoidance of undue concentration of economic power; (5) protection of depositors, investors, and customers from abuses or unsound banking practices; (6) promotion of a competitive, efficient financial system; and (7) compliance with laws and regulations.

There are real and apparent conflicts among some of these goals and the regulatory authorities have differences in priorities and in regulatory policies. In addition, a bank can choose which regulatory agency will supervise it and which policies govern it merely by the type of charter it receives. However, the key to understanding the U.S. bank regulatory system is the comprehensive, onsite examination of banks by a team of state or federal examiners who scrutinize banks' practices, procedures, policies, and assets and liabilities at least every 18 months.

Examination and supervision are intended to assure the prudential operation of banks and the appropriate management of risks inherent in banking. The examination process serves as a fact-gathering process about a bank's condition and the risks to which it is exposed, a tool of supervision, and ultimately, if required, for law enforcement. In 1986, the OCC decided to inaugurate a full-time surveillance system on the premises of 12 of the largest U.S. banks by installing live-in examiners to spot problems more quickly in light of troubled loan portfolios in an array of sectors, including international, oil and energy, agricultural, and real estate loans.[7]

The principal objectives of the examination are (1) to provide a thorough evaluation of a bank's condition; (2) to appraise management's quality and ability to establish and maintain adequate controls and sound policies; (3) to determine compliance with laws, rules, and regulations; and (4) to identify areas where corrective action is necessary to strengthen the bank and improve the quality of its operations.

Comprehensive on-site examinations focus on five key areas: (1) assessment of the bank's capital adequacy; (2) analysis of the bank's asset quality, with an emphasis on loans and investments; (3) evaluation of the bank's management, review of management policies, and assessment of internal and external control procedures; (4) analysis of the bank's profitability and the quality of its earnings; and (5) determination of the adequacy of the bank's liquidity, with an emphasis on asset and liability management policies and procedures.

Federal examiners rate banks on each of the five factors according to uniform principles and standards developed by the FFIEC. The rating system (which is known as the CAMEL rating for Capital adequacy, Asset quality, Management, Earnings, and Liquidity) produces numerical ratings for each of the five components and an overall composite rating. The composite rating is used to identify those banks in sound condition and those with weaknesses requiring closer supervisory attention.

In most cases, corrective action is taken before completion of the examination. An evaluation of bank activities is presented in a comprehensive written examination report. Examiner teams discuss with bank management overall conclusions and specific problems that have been discovered and meet with the board of directors to present their findings, criticisms, recommendations, and, in some cases, directives for change. The supervisory authority may, if necessary, initiate informal administrative action and require appropriate follow-up action. This generally involves a written agreement with the board of directors that prescribes necessary remedial actions.

If the directors fail to execute the directive, the agency can then take formal action, such as: (1) entering into formal agreements with the bank; (2) giving notice of charges; (3) presenting cease and desist orders; (4) assessing civil money penalties; and (5) removing officers or directors. Under law, the appropriate regulatory agency can issue a cease and desist order against a bank or any director, officer, employee, agent, or person participating in the conduct of affairs of the bank that the agency finds has committed a violation of law or has engaged in an unsafe and unsound practice. Current policies require that formal or informal administrative action must be taken against banks with certain composite ratings.

In addition to their formal enforcement powers and remedies, the agencies can employ civil and criminal sanctions of various kinds, some of which involve legal action through the courts. For example, if the directors of a national bank knowingly permit the management or employees of the bank to violate any of the provisions of the National Bank Act, all the ''rights, privileges, and franchises of the association'' may be terminated.[8] Every director who participates in or consents to a violation is personally liable "for all damages which the association, its shareholders, or any other person" may sustain as a result. In addition, the FDIC can terminate a bank's deposit insurance if it finds that the bank has engaged in violations of law or unsafe or unsound practices. The agencies can also use the leverage of pending corporate applications to encourage corrective action.

In addition to the commercial examination, specialized examinations are conducted for a number of activities, including international activities. The examination process is supplemented by remote computer-based systems that are designed to monitor the condition of banks between examinations and to serve as early warning systems to detect significant changes that may indicate anomalies or potential weaknesses. Efforts were recently completed to consolidate the systems of the three federal banking agencies and to coordinate a uniform approach to bank surveillance.

Responsibility for *supervising* the international activities of U.S. banks is divided, at the federal level, among the various banking agencies, similar to the domestic split. The FRB supervises the foreign activities of bank holding companies and their nonbank subsidiaries, as well as those of state member banks; the OCC supervises foreign activities of national banks; and the FDIC oversees foreign activities of U.S.-insured nonmember banks. The FRB, as the chartering agency, also has sole supervisory authority over all Edge Act Corporations, regardless of the Federal Reserve membership status of the corporation's parent bank. In the case of state-chartered banks, the chartering state also supervises the bank's international activities.

Since 1979 the OCC's Multinational Banking Division (MNB) has been responsible for supervising the global operations of the largest national banks, including examining their operations, monitoring and analyzing their activities, and reviewing their corporate applications. MNB monitors country risk within the national banking system, represents the OCC on the Interagency Country Exposure Review Committee, and serves as liaison with various foreign regulators and international organizations.

Although bank regulatory efforts have focused primarily on domestic operations, the examination of a U.S. bank's international division and activities does not differ conceptually from the regular commercial examination. However, it is often necessary to give special attention to bank assets and liabilities not found domestically and to different account procedures, laws, and regulations that may apply only abroad. The development of the Eurodollar market and the rise of sovereign lending that accompanied it have underscored the impact on domestic banks from international operations. The agencies typically use five methods to supervise the activities of foreign branches and subsidiaries of banks: (1) examination of branches on a remote basis from the head office; (2) examination of major branches in coordination with head office examinations; (3) examination of regional management centers; (4) supplemental examinations of individual branches or subsidiaries; and (5) remote examinations based on reports filed with U.S. banking authorities.

In addition to country risk, bank regulators also focus on such international activities as funds management and foreign exchange. Although there are no specific statutory or regulatory requirements relating to bank fund management, U.S. banking authorities are concerned about the heavy dependence of the larger U.S. banks on money market sources of funds. Their liquidity position is exposed to swings in market confidence and volatile money market rates, as the case of Continental Illinois vividly demonstrated in 1984. This is especially true for the banks operating internationally, where funds management involves managing liquidity and earnings in various countries and currencies.[9]

By their nature, banks tend to have short-term liabilities and longer-term assets, which expose them to interest rate and liquidity risks. The supervisory agencies review the banks' asset and liability maturity structures, their sources and concentrations of deposits, their interbank lending and placement activity, and their overall funds management practices in order to ensure prudent banking.

The primary supervisory approach to liquidity and funds management is to determine whether a bank's policies, practices, procedures, and controls are adequate and prudent. Liquidity is analyzed for each bank by assessing the maturity mismatch between assets and liabilities and its interest sensitivity position. An evaluation of liability liquidity involves the ability of the bank to attract funds when needed, at a reasonable cost, and with proper consideration given to maturity distribution. This mismatch placed international banks in a vulnerable position when their short-term deposits were used to generate longer-term loans to developing countries.

The examination process seeks to ascertain whether banks maintain adequate controls and procedures to manage the special risks arising from participation in the international interbank market, including the credit risk associated with each borrower/lender and the funding risk associated with mismatching maturities and providing continued access to markets. To analyze credit risk the examiners determine whether the bank has procedures to assess the creditworthiness of banks with which it is placing funds. Most banks have recently established an asset/liability management committee to set funds management policies and to centralize decision making.

Although U.S. bank regulatory agencies do not impose specific foreign exchange trading or position limits on commercial banks, they do review the banks' activities and policies to prevent undue risks and to ensure that adequate controls exist. The FFIEC developed a Uniform Guideline on Internal Control of Foreign Exchange in Commercial Banks to establish minimum standards for policy documentation, internal accounting controls, and audit documentation. The guidelines help bank management, auditors, and supervisory authorities evaluate a bank's internal control system for foreign exchange.

Examiners evaluate the quality and structure of international loan and investment portfolios, analyze foreign exchange activities, and assess the adequacy of internal controls and audit programs. International bank examinations also address country risk, foreign commercial credit, interbank dealing, and international operating systems. The bank regulatory agencies can take action if they identify problems and believe certain action is required.

COPING WITH COUNTRY RISK

Since the foreign loan exposure of major U.S. banks comprises a significant proportion of individual bank's assets, country risk evaluation has become an increasingly important concern for U.S. bank supervisors.[10] Because the high levels of foreign exposures by U.S. banks are a relatively recent occurrence, the U.S. banking agencies have only in the last few years established formal processes for analyzing country risk. The U.S. bank regulators evaluate country risk exposure not only for individual banks, but also to detect potential repayment difficulties that may result in nonperforming assets for U.S. banks.

Since 1978 the three federal bank regulatory agencies have used uniform examination procedures to evaluate and comment on the exposure of U.S. banks to debtor countries. The examination process includes a review of bank records and control systems. The examiners assess a bank's internal system for monitoring its country exposure and evaluate the adequacy of its country risk assessment and control system. A written report provides a basis for discussing and evaluating the bank's procedures for measuring country exposure, its system for establishing country lending limits, its capability for analyzing countries, and whether the bank adheres to its stated policies.

Since 1977 the agencies have been monitoring bank lending to foreign customers through a semiannual reporting system called the Country Lending Survey, required to be submitted by virtually every U.S. bank with a foreign office. Among other information, this report identifies the amount of credit extended to foreign parties by country and by type of foreign borrower, the remaining maturity of the asset, and the existence of any guarantor. Country exposures of U.S. branches of foreign banks are reviewed during the examination process.

Many critics have argued that the lack of adequate information, especially with respect to the rising country risk exposure and dramatic rise in short-term sovereign loans, was one of the most troublesome features of the global debt crisis. A number of efforts have been launched to improve the production and sharing of foreign lending information through the BIS and IMF, as well as private channels, such as the Institute for International Finance. In addition to making the Country Lending Survey a quarterly report, the "International Lending Supervision Act of 1983" requires banks to provide greater public information such as the identification of countries whose loans constitute more than 1 percent of the banks' assets.[11] In addition, by the end of 1985 the FFIEC will be seeking additional information from banks regarding their loans to foreign countries, to include specifying which loans are trade-financing credits and loans by U.S. branches of foreign banks to their home countries. This information is being sought in order to assess the creditworthiness of foreign loans. Furthermore, the FFIEC is seeking more detailed information on the maturity distributions of foreign loans, as an indication of the banks' exposure.[12]

All insured commercial banks and bank holding companies are required to submit certain reports to the federal supervisory agencies on a regular basis, many of which are available to the general public. The most fundamental financial report to all U.S. commercial banks is the Quarterly Report of Condition and Income (known as the Call Report). Although the level of detailed reporting requirements varies by the asset size of the bank and its exposure, a complete report consists of a balance sheet and income statement, along with supporting schedules that detail key items. For example, the reports identify loan valuation reserves, distribute the bank's major asset and liability accounts by maturity and type, show changes to its equity capital accounts, and summarize its loan loss experience. All bank holding companies must submit an annual report to the Federal Reserve and a 10-K report to the SEC. The Federal Reserve Board report contains financial information on each bank and nonbank subsidiary of the holding company and certain other data needed to monitor compliance with U.S. laws and regulations.

Monitoring and assessing country risk are done on a worldwide, consolidated basis, including significant bank and nonbank subsidiaries. As part of the monitoring process, the three federal banking agencies publish aggregate data showing (1) cross-border and nonlocal currency claims by residence of borrower; (2) cross-border and nonlocal currency claims on foreigners by country of guarantor; and (3) cross-border and nonlocal contingent claims. The report contains data on over 100 countries broken down by type of borrower (banks, public sector, and other private) and by maturity (one year and under, over one to five years, and over five years). The exposure is shown on the basis of external guarantees of the location of the head office banks. Information is also provided on commitments to advance funds and commitments that are guaranteed. The primary measure of exposure is the total cross-border and cross-currency loans and interbank placements with foreign borrowers adjusted for any guarantees from another country. This measure includes loans to customers in a foreign country by a U.S. bank, loans to customers in a different foreign country by a foreign branch of a U.S. bank or to customers in the country where the U.S. bank's foreign branch is located but where the loans are denominated in a nonlocal currency.

Since 1979 the three federal bank regulatory agencies have used the Interagency Country Exposure Review Committee (the Committee) to address the issue of country risk on a systematic basis. The Committee meets three times each year and has nine voting members, three from each agency. Before each meeting, agency personnel review economic studies prepared by the Federal Reserve on each of the countries selected for review, visit major multinational banks to review the country files and to discuss the selected countries with banks' economists and line officers, and review other sources of country data and assessments. At times the Committee may come under pressure from within the government not to make certain classification decisions because of the adverse impact they may have on other policy objectives with that country.

The banking regulatory agencies classify loans in a bank's portfolio as a means of assessing its condition. In reaction to the Domestic Housing and International Recovery and Stability Act of 1983, the banking regulators have strengthened their classification policy for international loans, replacing the previous categories of substandard, doubtful, and loss.[13] The new classifications of substandard, value-impaired, loss, and other transfer risk problems are intended to reflect the degree to which a country is not complying with the terms of its foreign debts, fails to adopt or comply with an IMF or other suitable adjustment program, and fails to adopt or comply with a bank rescheduling.

A loan classification of *substandard* is made when a country is not in compliance with its foreign debt obligations and is not adopting an economic adjustment or is not negotiating a viable rescheduling. A classification of *value-impaired* is given when more than one of the following conditions applies to a country: (1) has not fully paid its interest for six months; (2) has not complied with IMF programs; (3) has not met rescheduling terms for over one year; and (4) has not shown definite prospects for an orderly restoration of debt service in the near future. A *loss* classification is made when a loan is considered uncollectable and its value is so small that maintaining it as a bankable asset is not warranted. A country's outright repudiation of its foreign debt to its bank creditors is an example of an event that would give rise to a loss classification. The category of *other transfer risk problems* applies when a country (1) is not in compliance with foreign debt service obligations by remedying the situation by adopting economic adjustment measures; (2) is meeting its debt obligations but noncompliance seems imminent; or (3) has been previously classified but has resumed its debt service obligations on a sustained basis.

Since the supervisory focus is on identifying and limiting concentrations of credit, the Committee uses both qualitative and quantitative information and votes to rate countries as being strong, moderately strong, or weak, and, in extreme cases, to classify loans to a particular country. Since classification of credit to a country is an extreme measure, likely to affect the amount of credit U.S. banks will provide to it in the future, it is rarely used. This rating determines the level at which examiners mention concentrations of credit in the Examination Report. Countries not considered to be experiencing economic, social, or political problems of significance are rated *strong*. Those experiencing a limited number of economic, social, or political problems that are not presently of major concern are considered *moderately strong.* Those countries experiencing a number of economic, social, and political problems, or a significant problem considered correctable if remedial actions are taken in the near term, are rated *weak.*

Examiners generally comment in the Report of Examination on concentrations of loans to weak countries that exceed 5 percent of a bank's capital and on concentrations of loans to moderately strong countries if they exceed 10 percent of capital. Exposures to strong countries are commented on when exposure exceeds 25 percent of capital.

The risks involved in lending to foreign countries change constantly and require careful evaluation. Economic factors, the stability of the political system, the potential for social unrest, the management of a country's external and internal financial affairs, and other factors are evaluated when assessing the risk in lending to foreign borrowers. Consequently, the agencies try to balance the banking system's observations and conclusions with their own judgments, and stress portfolio diversification and adequate information systems for evaluating country risk. This regulatory country risk examination system has been criticized for its limited advisory function. Its purpose was to caution senior bank officials, and the agencies did not require specific country risk measures to be taken. Although this system provided major banks with information and guidance, its major objective was to encourage diversification in lending to developing countries and prevent problems before they occur. Nonetheless, the debt crisis did develop and placed even greater pressures on the bank regulators.

In an effort to buttress the role of the IMF as a "linchpin of the international financial system," the Reagan administration agreed to an increase in the IMF's resources.[14] It sought to make about $8.4 billion in additional funds available to the IMF, with about $5.8 billion for an increase in the U.S. quota and an additional $2.6 billion for the General Arrangements to Borrow. However, the Reagan administration confronted strong congressional sentiment that the international banks should pay a price for the additional funds. Many considered the IMF bill as little more than a "big bank bailout."

Others argued that, if anything, the bill was a debtor country bailout. A concerted effort, including sophisticated radio and television commercials, was made to defeat the bill. American Express Chairman James D. Robinson III commented on the charge that the IMF bill is a bank bailout bill as follows:

> The small town politician or bank in Maine says, "It serves those bastards right." I'd like to ask how many able-bodied men between the ages of 18 and 24 they have in their community and what size boots they wear. I'd tell them to get ready to go to Latin America because you let some of those governments go populist and you're going to have national security problems.[15]

Congress was aware that the global debt problem would require many years to resolve, would also require a high degree of cooperation and coordination among countries, and that the IMF quota increase, by itself, would not be sufficient to solve the problem. To cope with the longer-term problem, the House version of the IMF bill contained a number of provisions designed to "improve coordination among the industrialized nations, reduce the financial burdens on the developing nations and improve international banking supervision and regulation."[16] The IMF bill contained not only a series of measures intended to provide for greater supervision of international banking but also domestic housing legislation, compromises that were necessary to ensure its passage.

By adopting the Schumer amendment calling for the lengthening of the maturity of developing countries' debts at lower interest rate spreads, Congress also proposed a solution to the debt problem:

> A lengthening of the maturity of developing nation debt, where appropriate, would allow developing countries to use a greater percentage of their export earnings to finance national growth and additional imports. Currently, Mexico, Brazil, and Argentina are devoting more than one-third of their export earnings simply to pay interest on their outstanding loans. At this level, they have little chance of either repaying the principal or financing additional growth.[17]

Based on evidence presented in numerous hearings, congressional sentiment prompted action and legislation to deal with "the deficiencies in U.S. international bank regulation."[18] The House felt that the U.S. regulators had not demonstrated effective monitoring and had not prevented the "unsound operating and lending practices of U.S. banks"[19] and cited FDIC Chairman William Isaac's assessment:

> As bank supervisors, we failed to effectively caution American banks to refrain from foreign lending growth. Although portfolio concentrations were commented upon, sufficiently firm steps were not taken to limit concentrations and the leveraging of bank capital. Without question, our supervisory efforts need buttressing.[20]

Reacting to congressional pressure exerted as part of the price for passage of additional U.S. funding for the International Monetary Fund, and the shortfalls in their regulatory powers, the U.S. bank regulatory authorities proposed several reform measures to introduce greater discipline in international lending. Congress, with minor changes, accepted the recommendations proposed by the bank regulatory agencies to deal with international lending. This was also done in recognition of the overextension of sovereign and foreign lending beyond prudent limits and the lack of adequate provisioning, that is, setting aside reserves for possible loan losses, for foreign loans.

In an April 1983 joint memorandum, the Federal Reserve, FDIC, and Office of the Comptroller of the Currency explicitly recognized the "transfer risk" associated with sovereign lending caused by the possibility that a borrower may not be able to maintain debt servicing in the currency in which the debt is to be repaid because of a lack of foreign exchange. The three federal bank regulatory agencies proposed a five-point plan of regulation that would:

1. Strengthen the existing program of country risk evaluation and examination, including stricter capital adequacy requirements for those banks having large concentrations of credit in particular countries;
2. Increase public disclosure of the country exposure of banks, including more frequent and more timely availability of aggregate data and public disclosure by individual banks of all country exposure concentrations;
3. Formalize and make uniform a system for reserving against certain country exposures (discussed in more detail below);
4. Change and make uniform the way income is reported from international loan fees; and
5. Increase international cooperation among foreign banking regulators and provide for greater sharing of IMF information.[21]

These proposals, which became law with passage of the Domestic Housing and International Recovery and Financial Stability Act in November 1983, specifically do not include country lending limits, on the argument that country differences, political pressures, and the already high exposure of some banks in some countries rule out such ceilings. Since the loan concentration of leading U.S. banks was limited to a few debtor countries, the establishment of effective country lending limits would have prevented the major U.S. banks from extending additional financing to these debtors at their moment of greatest need. Preexisting federal and state laws in the United States, however, do limit the amount a bank can lend to one borrower generally to 15 percent of the bank's capital. In 1979 the comptroller of the currency ruled that foreign governments and their related entities came under this restriction and that loans to foreign government agencies and instrumentalities should be combined with loans to the central government for purposes of this lending limit unless (1) the borrower has resources or revenue of its own sufficient to service its debt obligations (the "means" test), and (2) the loan is obtained for a purpose consistent with the borrower's general business (the "purpose" test).

In December 1983 the Comptroller of the Currency, and the other bank regulatory authorities, issued proposed rules that provide a uniform method to require banks to establish special reserves against international assets that have not been serviced over a protracted period of time.[22] This proposal would implement a requirement of section 905(a) of the International Lending Supervision Act of 1983 providing that the appropriate federal banking agency require banks to maintain a special reserve whenever, in the agency's judgment, the quality of a banks' assets has been impaired by a protracted inability of public or private borrowers in a foreign country to make payments on their external debt or where no definitive prospects exist for the orderly restoration of debt service.

The act requires these reserves be charged against current income and not be considered as part of capital or allowance for possible loan losses. Interestingly, the regulators also noted that, under certain circumstances, additional lending may improve the quality of outstanding loans.

> In implementing the provisions of the International Lending Supervision Act of 1983 the agencies recognize the importance to the stability of both the international banking system and world economy of providing continued international flows of bank credit in the periods ahead, especially to countries implementing IMF-approved economic adjustment programs designed to correct the countries' economic difficulties in an orderly manner. Such new flows under appropriate circumstances may strengthen the functioning of the adjustment process, help to improve the quality of outstanding credit, and thus may be consistent with the objectives of the program of improved supervision of international lending . . . . [23]

Banks are now required to establish "Allocated Transfer Risk Reserves" (ATRR) against assets that are found to be impaired by transfer risk problems that result in a protracted inability of debtor countries to repay their debts. While the percentage amount of reserves required for specific assets has not yet been determined, guidelines in the proposed regulations suggest an average of 10 percent of the principal amount of the asset for the first year. Since some countries (such as Zaire, Poland, Bolivia, Nicaragua and Sudan) have already exhibited severe debt service problems over a number of years, the initial reserves established under this plan for countries like these may be substantially higher than 10 percent.[24] Additional reserves may be required in subsequent years, usually in increments of 15 percent of the principal amount of the asset. The specific amount and timing of the reserve requirement will vary by country and, in some cases, by the type of asset. However, the percentage reserve for specific assets and countries would be uniform for all banks. The federal bank regulators also require that loans that are more than 90 days overdue be listed as nonperforming and be placed on a "nonaccruing" basis. Accordingly, a bank cannot count any unpaid interest as income and must reduce previous amounts included in income. A number of major U.S. banks began to feel the impact on their earnings from Argentina's overdue loans since 1984.

The sensitive nature of loan ratings was underscored by the activity surrounding Argentina's payment of certain arrears shortly before the ICERC's meeting in June 1985. Many bankers and government officials feared the consequences of loans to Argentina being classified substandard or value-impaired. The psychological impact on the market's reaction and erosion of confidence in the capital markets was of major concern to regulators and policymakers. Argentina's June 1985 financing package and agreement with the IMF averted adverse action by the regulators.[25] Peru's loan rating had also been widely expected to be lowered to value-impaired during the course of the ICERC's deliberations, but its rating was kept at substandard reportedly because of political considerations in order not to antagonize the country's president-elect, Alan Garcia Perez.[26]

Some may argue that these reforms are inadequate in light of the present state of international bank lending, especially the exposure to developing countries. However, these reforms are a balanced attempt to rectify the recent over-extension in international lending by requiring higher capital ratios and loan loss reserves without adopting regulatory overkill that might risk aggravating the international financial markets and exacerbating the global debt problem.

Progress has been made toward developing ways for the supervisory authorities to catch up with the internationalization of banking, although the roles of the world's supervisory authorities may need to be clarified to ensure confidence in the global financial markets. Whether the greater supervision, tightening of the rules, and greater cooperation by bank regulators will be a sufficient contribution to the resolution of the debt crisis through a more realistic reflection of the status of a bank's international loans, the prudent extensions of new credits, and loan reschedulings where necessary, remains to be seen.

INTERNATIONAL COOPERATION

With the rise of international lending during the 1970s, representatives from bank supervisory agencies of the major industrial countries began to meet to discuss cooperative initiatives and to exchange information.[27] In 1974 the governors of the central banks of the Group of Ten countries formed the BIS Committee on Banking Regulations and Supervisory Practices (also known as the Cooke Committee). In addition to the Concordat discussed below, the Cooke Committee reached agreement on the following: (1) consolidation of accounting on a worldwide basis so that parent bank supervisors can monitor a bank's country risk exposure (several countries have enacted this into law); (2) collection of BIS data on the maturity structure of loans and on country exposure; and (3) cooperation among supervisory authorities to provide for sharing of information and to allow for inspections by parent bank authorities of their banks' foreign entities in some cases.

One of the Cooke Committee's major efforts has been in the area of developing rules for a lender of last resort in international banking. The function of a lender of last resort is to maintain public confidence, a critical ingredient in domestic and international banking.[28] Any actual or potential insolvency of a large bank can shatter public confidence in the overall financial system. The extent of disruption in the system depends on how quickly the lack of confidence spreads throughout the financial markets. In addition, the extent of the loss of confidence hinges on the public's perception of whether there is an institution with the capability to provide enough liquidity or capital to the banking system. If a capable institution is not available in the financial markets, and the public (that is, depositors, investors, other banks) perceives this deficiency, then the government, as the ultimate lender of last resort, may have no choice but to intervene. The onus would then fall on the government as lender of last resort to act quickly and effectively.

In the United States the Federal Reserve Bank (FRB), through its discount window, serves as the lender of last resort, while the FDIC provides deposit insurance and is involved in handling distressed or failing banks. Deposit insurance is intended both to protect individual depositors and to promote system stability by maintaining individual and market confidence. Deposit insurance programs in the United States are provided by the Federal Deposit Insurance Corporation (FDIC), the Federal Savings and Loan Insurance Corporation (FSLIC), the National Credit Union Administration (NCUA), and several state agencies. At present, federal insurance covers domestic deposits up to $100,000.

About 98 percent of all U.S. commercial banks have FDIC insurance. In addition, the laws of all but three states require insurance as a prerequisite to receiving a state charter. Finally, market factors and public acceptance effectively demand that bank deposits be insured, and recent events in Ohio and Maryland underscore the shift in favor of federal insurance.

The bank supervisory agencies handle distressed or failing banks in several ways, as the rescue of Continental Illinois in July 1984 demonstrated, thereby raising the possibility of a precedent for handling banking problems caused by international loans. First, the regulatory authority attempts to get the existing stockholders or other parties to inject capital into the bank. If this cannot be accomplished, the regulatory agency tries to encourage or arrange a merger with a healthy institution. Should neither of these remedies be possible, and it is evident that the bank cannot resolve its problems, the FDIC becomes involved. The agencies seek the solution that causes the least disruption to the banking system and the community concerned, and that minimizes the cost to the FDIC.

The FDIC, in turn, has several options. First, it may extend financial assistance to a bank to prevent its closing. It can only do so, however, if the bank is judged to be essential to provide adequate banking service to the community. This remedy has been rarely used, most notably for the Bank of the Commonwealth in 1971, First Pennsylvania Bank, N.A. in 1980, and Continental Illinois in 1984. Second, the FDIC may close the bank and arrange a purchase of assets and assumption of liabilities by another bank. To arrange for such a transaction, the FDIC may provide financial assistance to the acquiring bank. In a purchase and assumption transaction all of the closed bank's depositors and creditors are fully protected. Franklin National Bank's closing was handled by the FDIC using this option. Third, a more drastic option is to close the bank and pay off the insured depositors. Perhaps because of the danger of exhausting the liquidity of the deposit insurance fund, the largest bank whose deposits were paid off had only about $70 million in total assets. Fourth, a seldom used option is to establish a Deposit Insurance National Bank (DINB) to acquire the closed bank. However, a DINB can only operate for two years and then it must be liquidated if the stockholders of the closed bank are unable to capitalize the DINB.

The deposit insurance mechanism has been extraordinarily effective in maintaining confidence and forestalling panics, although recently state insurance programs in Ohio and Maryland did not fulfill those roles well. This fact has been underscored by numerous economists, including John Kenneth Galbraith who observed that FDIC had succeeded in developing into an utterly reliable lender of last resort. Even though a massive default by major debtor countries would be greater than the FDIC's limited insurance resources of about $18 billion (with some $4 billion tied up with Continental Illinois), the full faith and credit of the United States could back the FDIC's commitment.

By limiting bank failures, a lender of last resort facility serves as one means of achieving the goal of promoting economic stability. The function of the FRB's discount window is to provide liquidity to depository institutions to meet seasonal credit needs or unanticipated needs for funds, such as one that might result from the repudiation of outstanding loans to major borrowing countries. Short-term assistance to banks, which for various reasons may have lost access to other sources of funds, provides an otherwise sound institution with a temporary means to make needed corrections or respond to shocks beyond its control. When in rare emergency situations institutions experience liquidity problems, the Federal Reserve may extend credit on a longer-than-temporary basis in its role as lender of last resort. When providing funds, the FRB requires that the loans be fully collateralized and, in "emergency" cases, that the borrower develop and implement a plan to resolve its problems.

In international lending, there is ambiguity as to whether the central bank of the host country or the central bank of the parent country bears the responsibility for acting as the lender of last resort for a *subsidiary* of a foreign bank. In the case of foreign *branches*, there is no ambiguity because the parent bank is legally responsible for its branches and, if it gets into trouble, the parent bank's central bank is responsible. These principles of international bank supervision were originally set down by the central bank governors of the group of ten countries and Switzerland in what is known as the Basle Concordat of 1975, as follows:

1. The supervision of foreign banking establishments is the joint responsibility of parent and host authorities.
2. No foreign banking establishment should escape supervision.
3. The supervision of liquidity should be the primary responsibility of the host authorities.
4. The supervision of solvency is essentially a matter for the parent authority in the case of foreign branches and primarily the responsibility of the host authority in the case of foreign subsidiaries.
5. Practical cooperation should be provided by the exchange of information between host and parent authorities and by the authorization of bank inspectors by or on behalf of parent authorities on the territory of the host authority.[29]

While this Concordat represented an important step toward cooperation by international supervisory authorities for coping with the proliferation of international lending, it suffered from several weaknesses. First, by giving primary responsibility to the host authority for the supervision of the solvency of foreign subsidiaries, the Concordat ran counter to a recommendation by the central bank governors that banks should be supervised by home country authorities on a consolidated global basis. The danger was that the host country might look to the parent authorities to supervise the foreign subsidiaries located in their countries under consolidated supervision, while home country authorities could rely on a host country's supervisory responsibility accorded by the Concordat.

Furthermore, the 1975 Concordat led to a widespread mistaken understanding by commercial bankers that the supervisory and lender of last resort responsibilities of national authorities were intertwined. In fact, it was never intended that the Concordat would establish guidelines for lender of last resort responsibilities. However, the financial markets inferred that a central bank was responsible in a lender of last resort sense for banks falling within its supervisory jurisdiction.

These weaknesses became readily apparent in the events surrounding the collapse of Banco Ambrosiano's Luxembourg subsidiary in the summer of 1982. Both the Luxembourg and Italian authorities refused responsibility for supervising or providing lender of last resort facility to the Luxembourg subsidiary, primarily because legally it was a holding company rather than a bank. The Italian authorities believed they had limited responsibility for a foreign subsidiary because its activities were beyond its control. The Luxembourg authorities felt that the local subsidiary of a foreign bank that was doing business under its parent's name should be supported by the parent and, if needed, by the parent's central bank.

The Banco Ambrosiano controversy was one of the key factors prompting a revision of the Concordat by the central bank governors in June 1983. This revision introduced clearer guidelines for the supervision of holding companies. The new Concordat expressed the principle of consolidated supervision. That is, parent authorities should supervise risks on the basis of a bank's global operations. While under the original Concordat the primary responsibility for supervising the solvency of foreign subsidiaries was carried by the host authority, under the new Concordat this is a joint responsibility of the host and parent authority. Under these guidelines Italian authorities would have been responsible for ensuring that a holding company such as Ambrosiano's Luxembourg subsidiary would be covered by adequate supervision or the parent bank would be prohibited from operating such a subsidiary.[30]

The 1983 Concordat declares that it does not address the lender of last resort function. As in the past, central banks prefer to remain silent, or say little, about their willingness to provide lender of last resort support, to avoid encouraging excessive risk taking by banks. Declaring a division of lender responsibilities would also hamper efforts to improve bank supervision in some offshore banking centers. However, if banking authorities are too reticent about offering lender of last resort assistance, international banks might operate on the false assumption that such assistance would indeed be available.

The new Concordat appears to have been accompanied by a shift in the U.S. position on lender of last resort responsibilities. U.S. authorities had been reluctant to offer lender of last resort assistance to foreign subsidiaries of U.S. banks. However, in a May 1983 speech Henry Wallich, a governor of the Federal Reserve Board, expressed the willingness of the Federal Reserve, under appropriate circumstances, to support foreign subsidiaries of U.S. banks, provided the parent institution is itself solvent. "By the nature of relationships in international banking, the principle of parental responsibility applies. Branches *and subsidiaries* of foreign parents must first look to these parents in case of liquidity needs, while the parents look to their own central banks."[31]

In March 1986, the U.S. bank regulators adopted a plan to relieve the pressure on banks serving the hard-pressed U.S. farm industry by providing "breathing space" through a more liberal accounting treatment for renegotiated problem loans.[32] The key elements of the plan include:

1. Allowing a bank "experiencing difficulties to operate below the minimum capital requirement provided the bank has the capacity to restore capital within five years";
2. Not discouraging banks from forebearing on farm loans, recognizing that a restructuring may be in the interests of the bank and the borrower when "there is a reasonable prospect that the borrower will eventually be able to repay the loan"; and perhaps most importantly,
3. Not requiring an "automatic charge-off of loans that have been restructured. Generally accepted accounting principles, as set forth in Financial Accounting Standard No. 15 (Accounting by Debtors and Creditors for Troubled Debt Restructurings), allow financial institutions to maintain the value of a restructured credit provided that the total of anticipated future cash receipts under the new modified terms which are both probable and can be reasonably estimated at least equals the principal value of the loan. Thus generally accepted accounting principles do not necessarily require the immediate charge-off of loans or portions of loans that have been restructured in accordance with that rule."[33]

In making this announcement, the regulators indicated that they could be extended to cover other banks serving troubled sectors. With respect to the banks' vulnerability to the problems facing debtor countries, the application of Federal Accounting Standards Board Rule 15 (FASB 15) could create some difficulties. For example, in the negotiations process the debtor countries could try to seek significantly better terms if they believed that their creditor banks would be permitted to use FASB 15 for such loans.

Through various means, bank regulatory agencies have sought to buttress public confidence in the ability of the banking systems to cope with the impact of the international debt crisis. Although bank regulators have had problems grappling with the dramatic rise in international lending, they have recently increased the capital rates for the industry to 6 percent, with even higher ratios required for some individual banks—with calls by bank regulators that it be increased to 9 percent.[34] In addition, in an October 30, 1985 banking circular to national banks, the OCC noted the banks' troubled loan exposure to developing countries as well as in the domestic market. The circular admonished banks for paying out excess cash dividends when retained earnings have often not kept pace with the higher level of volatility and risk experienced by the banks in the current economic environment.

> Cash dividends represent a distribution of net income. They should bear a direct correlation to the level of the bank's current and expected earning stream, the bank's need to maintain an adequate capital base, and the marketplace's perception of the bank—not the financial expectations of bank shareholders. Paying dividends that deplete a bank's capital base to an inadequate level constitutes an unsafe and unsound banking practice.[35]

There have also been suggestions that banks be required to establish reserve requirements against transfer risks based on the percentage of primary capital that their exposure to certain countries comprises. Accompanying efforts to require greater loan-loss reserves have confronted U.S. tax rules that provide U.S. banks with little benefit in maintaining reserves against troubled foreign loans. This is in contrast to the European system, which often encourages provisions for questionable foreign loans through "hidden reserves," a practice not allowed in the United States. As a result, European banks have been writing off their doubtful assets since the onset of the debt crisis and have been critical of the failure of leading U.S. banks to do likewise. Indeed, the U.S. bank regulators have noted their opposition to the proposed elimination of the special deduction banks receive for bad debt reserves contained in the tax reform bill. The basis for this opposition stems from the view that banks should be encouraged to maintain and build adequate loan-loss reserves as a means of promoting the safety and soundness of financial institutions.[36]

Even though some observers had concluded by the beginning of 1985 that the debt crisis was "all but over,"[37] bank regulators have since adopted a more cautious, if not pessimistic, assessment. They recognize the potential fragility of these debtor countries' loans, the potential impact on bank earnings, and the erosion of public confidence prompted by the international debt crisis. According to a senior bank regulator, banks have been more willing to reserve against possible international loan losses despite the impact on earnings because they moved from a philosophy that "countries don't go broke to a philosophy that loans to [developing] countries may be bad."[38] Many U.S. regional banks and small European banks have opted to cut back their foreign loans after establishing loan loss reserves or writing off their loans to debtor countries. Some officials have suggested that the commercial banks should use the next few years to reserve against these loans because they will have to be written off in the not-too-distant future. Whether this is an accurate assessment remains to be seen.

The perception among European banks that U.S. banks are fudging their books with respect to international loans is as worrisome as their perception regarding the unhealthy state of the U.S. banking system. With increased pressures for banks to reflect a realistic accounting of the value of their troubled foreign loans, bank regulators will play a key role in determining how potential future developments are treated. Since major banks have been more active in arranging loan swaps of foreign borrowers, the issue has arisen regarding how to treat the loans recorded by the banks. The American Institute of Certified Public Accountants (AICPA) and the Office of the Comptroller of the Currency have issued guidelines providing that the banks engaging in loan swaps be required to prove that the loans they swapped are worth the full amount of the loan. Otherwise the bank must recognize its loss on the transaction and reduce its earnings, a step that could make U.S. banks less competitive in this area and discourage their use of such transactions.[39] In addition, alternative debt relief schemes, such as interest capping and capitalization of interest, would require decisions by bank regulators about when to recognize earnings.

Whether efforts aimed at encouraging increased commercial bank lending to the debtor countries will lead to the easing of the U.S. bank regulatory scheme remains to be seen. In any event the tension between assuring soundness and safety of U.S. banks and the need for additional capital by the debtor countries remain at the core of the problem. In addition, bank regulators may have a certain degree of flexibility in dealing with a bank's treatment of a debtor country's "conciliatory default" or unilateral rescheduling formula, although, in light of the Allied case, it is not clear to what degree such a development could be fruitful.[40] Their flexibility would appear to be much more constrained if a debtor country undertakes an outright repudiation of its foreign loan obligations.[41]

NOTES

1. Graeme Rutledge and Geoffrey Bell, "Facing Reality on Sovereign Debt," *Euromoney*, November 1984, p. 105.

2. "U.S. Won't Let Biggest Bank in Nation Fail," *The Wall Street Journal*, September 20, 1984.

3. Robert E. Weintraub, *International Lending by U.S. Banks: Practices, Problems, and Policies* (Fairfax: George Mason University, 1983).

4. Gary Hector, "The True Face of Bank Earnings," *Fortune*, April 16, 1984, p. 82.

5. *The Wall Street Journal*, "Large Banks Are Hit by New Set of Rumors and Stock Prices Fall," September 25, 1984.

6. Richard Dale, *Bank Supervision Around the World* (New York: Group of Thirty, 1982).

7. Eleanor Johnson Tracy, "Living With the Live-In Bank Examiner," *Fortune*, March 3, 1986.

8. Weintraub, op cit., p. 10.

9. Bank for International Settlements, *The International Interbank Market* (Basle: BIS, 1983).

10. Irving Friedman, *The World Debt Dilemma: Managing Country Risks* (Washington, D.C. and Philadelphia: Council for International Banking Studies and Robert Morris Associates, 1983), ch. 16.

11. See Karin Lissakers, "Bank Regulation and International Debt" in Richard E. Feinberg and Valeriana Kallab (eds.), *Uncertain Future: Commercial Banks and the Third World* (New Brunswick, New Jersey: Transaction Books, 1984).

12. Monica Langley, "Bank Regulators Ask for More Data on Foreign Loans," *The Wall Street Journal,* October 8, 1985.

13. Robert R. Bench, *A Framework and New Techniques for International Bank Supervision* (Washington, D.C.: Office of the Comptroller of the Currency, 1982).

14. Remarks of Ronald Reagan at the Annual Meeting of the Board of Governors, *Presidential Documents,* October 3, 1983, p. 1337.

15. As quoted in Peter Brimelow, "Why the U.S. Shouldn't Fill the IMF's Till," *Fortune,* November 14, 1983, p. 58.

16. International Recovery and Financial Stability Act, House of Representatives, Report No. 98-175, 98th Congress, 1st Session, May 16, 1983, p. 21.

17. Ibid.

18. Ibid.

19. Ibid., p. 30.

20. Ibid., p. 31.

21. Federal Reserve Bank of Governors, Federal Deposit Insurance Corporation, and Office of the Comptroller of the Currency, *Joint Memorandum Program for Improved Supervision and Regulation of International Lending,* April 7, 1983.

22. Federal Deposit Insurance Corporation, Office of the Comptroller of the Currency, and Board of Governors of the Federal Reserve System, *Interagency Statement on Examination Treatment of International Loans,* December 15, 1983.

23. Ibid. Also see Cynthia C. Lichtenstein, "U.S. Response to the International Debt Crisis: The International Lending Supervision Act of 1983 and the Regulations Issued Under the Act," in William N. Eskridge, Jr. (ed.), *A Dance Along the Precipice* (Lexington, Massachusetts: Lexington Books, 1985).

24. Andrew Albert, "Fed Adopts Foreign Loan Reserves," *The American Banker,* February 3, 1984.

25. Donald Shoultz, "Monetary Fund Leader Backing Argentine Plan," *The American Banker,* June 12, 1985.

26. *The New York Times,* "Debt Downgrading for Peru Is Feared," June 3, 1985; ibid., "Ratings Stable for Latin Debt," June 24, 1985.

27. G.G. Johnson with Richard K. Abrams, *Aspects of the International Banking Safety Net* (Washington, D.C.: International Monetary Fund, March 1983).

28. Jack Guttentag and Richard Herring, *The Lender-of-Last Resort Function in an International Context* (Princeton, New Jersey: Princeton University, 1983).

29. Richard Dale, "Basle Concordat: Lessons from Ambrosiano," *The Banker,* September 1983, p. 55.

30. Ibid.

31. Henry C. Wallich, "Central Banks as Regulators and Lenders of Last Resort in an International Context: A View From the United States," in *Key Issues in International Banking,* Federal Reserve Bank of Boston, 1978.

32. *Joint Statement of the Federal Reserve Board, the Federal Deposit Insurance Corporation, and the Office of the Comptroller of the Currency on Regulatory Policies Toward Agricultural Lenders;* William Hall, "U.S. Accounting Rules Relaxed to Help Banks Over Loan Crisis," *The Financial Times,* March 13, 1986; Bartlett Naylor, "Bank Regulators Relax Capital Rules for Troubled Farm, Energy Lenders," *The American Banker,* March 28, 1986.

33. Joint Statement of the Federal Reserve Board, the Federal Deposit Insurance Corporation, and the Office of the Comptroller of the Currency on Regulatory Policies Toward Agricultural Lenders.

34. Barbara Durr, "Comptroller's Office Nudges Banks to Boost Their Loan Loss Reserves," *The American Banker*, February 4, 1985.

35. Comptroller of the Currency, *Banking Circular, Dividends,* Washington, D.C.: Office of the Comptroller of the Currency, October 30, 1985.

36. Alan Murray, "Volcker Again Backs Tax Break on Loan Reserves," *The Wall Street Journal*, April 3, 1986.

37. Nicholas D. Kristof, "Debt Crisis Called All but Over," The New York *Times*, February 4, 1985.

38. As quoted in Hector, op. cit., p. 82.

39. Comptroller of the Currency, *Banking Circular, Accounting for Loan Swaps,* Washington, D.C.: Office of the Comptroller of the Currency, May 22, 1985.

40. *Allied Bank International* v. *Banco Credito Agricola De Cartago,* United States Court of Appeals for the Second Circuit, May 18, 1985.

41. See Anatole Kaletsky, *The Costs of Default* (New York: Priority Press Publications, 1985).

5

Conclusion: Managing the Debt Crisis and Proposed Alternative Solutions

In conducting foreign policy, decision makers have traditionally specialized in national security issues, particularly the political and military dimensions. International financial issues have usually been left to the discretion of the respective finance ministeries. However, the foreign policy, national security, and political spillover from the global debt problem are beginning to emerge in clearer form. "The dilemma for Latin America is how to reconcile the stiff austerity programs required by the International Monetary Fund with rising popular demands for relief from negative economic growth and widespread distress."[1]

The U.S. government had ample interests at stake to motivate it to take action when the 1982 debt crisis struck. American banks have the largest exposure in Latin America, and the United States has special economic and security interests in the region. A loss of confidence in the ability of key Latin American debtors to service their debt obligations was permeating commercial banks and casting an ominous cloud over the banking system.

Using its Exchange Stabilization Fund (ESF), the U.S. Treasury Department entered into several swap agreements—an arrangement between two parties to exchange a certain amount of one currency for another and to reverse the transaction at a specified date—with a number of key debtor countries. By spearheading efforts to provide short-term financing to Mexico and Brazil during the summer and fall of 1982, as well as for Argentina in 1984 and 1985, the U.S. government obtained a key ingredient—time. The ESF also agreed to be substituted for the claims of the Bank for International Settlements, in certain transactions, in the event a country were not to fulfill its obligations to the BIS. A fundamental objective of the short-term nature of ESF financing is to support the IMF's role as the primary source of official medium-term balance-of-payments financing. This has been an essential function in light of the gap in time between a country's turning to the IMF for assistance and the availability of such resources.

Concerned about an orderly resolution of the debt problem, worried about its ramifications for key Latin American states, cognizant of the sensitivity of its own recovery, and aware of its reliance on exports, the United States government in late 1982 began to implement a plan, subsequently approved at the Williamsburg summit in July 1983. Although the plan has come under increasing attack and has been modified by the Baker Plan of October 1985, the United States has not abandoned the following five key elements of this strategy:

1. Effective adjustment in borrowing countries, including not increasing imports beyond affordable level, stimulating exports and adopting other measures to eliminate distortions and inefficiencies in their domestic economy;
2. Continued availability of official balance-of-payments financing in support of adjustment measures, with the IMF serving as the key institution for this purpose;
3. Willingness of governments and central banks in lending countries to act quickly in response to liquidity emergencies in selected cases;
4. Continued commercial bank lending to countries pursuing sound adjustment programs; and
5. Restoration of sustainable economic growth and preservation and strengthening of the free trading system.[2]

Efforts by several debtor countries to implement austerity programs to service their debt obligations and maintain their creditworthiness have led to economic hardship for the local population and resulted in political protests and violence. In part, this has been sparked by significant income reductions and raised concern about the possibility that such economic deterioration will provide a fertile atmosphere for radical nationalism and anti-Americanism, especially as the perception sets in that the austerity sacrifices are being made to maintain the well-being of the"gringo banks." Therefore, international bankers and national security decision makers are likely to grapple with these international financial issues well into the foreseeable future as efforts are undertaken to stimulate growth and development.

Assessments regarding the likelihood of a favorable outcome to the global debt problem range from extreme pessimism to outright optimism. Optimists tend to view the current difficulties as a temporary liquidity shortage that can be alleviated by growth in the industrial world, a resulting increase in debtor countries' commodity prices, and moderate interest rates. This school of thought also regards protectionism as one of the major obstacles to a favorable resolution of the debt problem. Pessimists often view the problem as a matter of solvency and conclude that debtor countries have little, if any, reasonable expectation of ever making payments either on or of their onerous debts. Accordingly, this school of thought considers the financial rescue packages as little more than pouring new debt on top of old and making the debt burden tougher to bear. This assessment often leads to a search for alternative means to alleviate the debt burden of the major debtors, especially through a form of debt relief.[3] The differing assessments of those evaluating the foreign debt of developing countries and their prospects may be explained by a basic difference in outlook. An optimist observes: "Well, things just can't get any worse"; the pessimist responds: "Oh yeah, just wait." The following World Bank assessment represents a middle ground:

> Assuming an intelligent response to current problems, it is likely that the crisis can be weathered without serious disruption to the international financial system. Unfortunately, the measures taken by many developing countries to restrain their borrowing have been, and will continue to be, extremely painful. Austerity programs and attempts to achieve trade surpluses are exacting a heavy toll.[4]

Government officials involved in international economic issues agree that the means employed thus far to cope with the debt issue can be improved. Reliance on a robust recovery in the industrialized countries and a dramatic expansion of world trade to provide the solution to the global debt problem highlights the need for policy coordination between trade and finance ministers, a task that remains largely unimplemented.[5]

Actions taken by the creditors have been designed to provide time—assumed to be the key ingredient needed by the debtor countries—to recover.[6] The industrialized countries have pinned their hopes on a global economic recovery that, when combined with debtor countries' domestic adjustment, will provide debtors with sufficient hard currency earnings to make their debt service obligations more manageable. Indeed, a basis for concluding that the problem is a liquidity crunch stems, in part, from assessments that economic growth in the industrial countries will pull the debtor countries out of their current, but temporary, financial woes.

Despite the sharp decline of the dollar in 1986, the fall of real interest rates, and the fairly strong growth of the economies of the industrialized countries, Jacque de Larosiere, the executive director of the IMF, has expressed reservations about the systemic problems posed by the global economic environment. He has emphasized that the financing gaps facing such oil exporters as Mexico are confronting the international system with a challenge that requires more than has been offered by the Baker Plan.[7] The IMF has also criticized the United States for its large budget deficits, yet through its $150 billion trade deficit the United States has absorbed $50 billion of debtor countries' exports annually for the past several years.

Latin America has experienced the brunt of the debt problem. The adjustment process for the major debtors has relied on both internal and external factors. Domestic efforts aimed at attaining stable exchange rates and fighting inflation have not been successful, although Argentina and Brazil have taken significant steps since 1985. Most of the adjustment has consisted of dramatic cuts in imports as efforts to expand exports have been dependent on world economic growth that has not fulfilled expectations. Since exports are vital to the debt-servicing capabilities of the debtor countries, renewed calls for protectionism in industrialized countries generate concerns over their ability to generate foreign exchange earnings. Combined with the uncertainty surrounding growth in the industrialized countries, the prospects for Latin American export growth remain murky. Even with the easing of the debt burden through reschedulings and the reduction of interest rates and spreads charged to debtor countries, in 1985 Latin American countries were spending over one-third of their export earnings to service their interest payments alone and over two-thirds when the amortization of long-term debt is included.[8] Yet even with such burden, the debtors have little choice but to adopt measures to reestablish their creditworthiness by creating a stable economic and political environment that is noninflationary and encourages domestic savings and investment.

TRADE AND DEVELOPMENT

Long-term U.S. policy efforts toward alleviating the debt crisis have been largely premised on trade and growth as the vehicles for its satisfactory resolution. Proponents of this position argue that reinforcing the recovery of the developed countries benefits the developing countries, yielding a mutually reinforcing process. Nonetheless, the fragile nature of this strategy is reflected in remarks of the deputy secretary of state following completion of the 1984 Argentine financial package. "The focus of our attention is shifting from insuring immediate liquidity to promoting long-term growth. Without renewed real growth, debtor nations will lurch from one short-term crisis to another."[9]

International trade is a means of earning foreign exchange and for employing comparative advantage. Although numerous factors have contributed to the debt problem, many argue that "the deterioration of trade has perhaps been the single most important factor."[10] Trade expansion, including the specialization it fosters, has been used by developing countries to earn foreign exchange and leverage borrowing capacity. However, as debtor countries' obligations increased, their inability to generate sufficient foreign exchange through international trade eroded their creditworthiness.

The key role of exports and growth for developed countries has been widely recognized. Industrialized countries have been urged to relieve the foreign debt pressures by providing borrowing countries with time and a favorable international trading environment by alleviating the dangers of protectionism: "In our interest we must give developing countries a fair chance to expand their exports. After all, if we cannot be paid in cash, why refuse to be paid in kind?"[11]

Raised by the former president of the Bank for International Settlements, this question does reflect an awareness of the rise of barter and countertrade transactions in international trade. Spurred by the needs of developing countries at a time of severe financing difficulties, barter and countertrade have developed in response to a specific problem, as an alternative to financing imports and as a means of increasing exports. Estimates of the extent of such trade vary markedly, ranging from 5 to 40 percent of international trade, with 20 percent a frequently cited figure. Critics of barter and countertrade argue that it erodes free international trade by emphasizing bilateral rather than multilateral arrangements. Few, however, dispute its attractiveness to debtor countries in severe financial straits. Indeed, Peru has reportedly offered a deal to Bank of America, its third-largest creditor, whereby the bank would act as a broker to find buyers for Peruvian goods in order to be paid in dollars for the bank's outstanding loans.[12] Whether these arrangements will disappear when the debt problem is ameliorated or will beome a permanent part of the international trading system remains to be seen.

In light of the factors contributing to the harshness of the global debt problem, it is not surprising that the industrial countries have looked to economic growth as the means of alleviating the problem and providing the debtor countries with hope. Although there is increasing awareness that, by itself, economic growth cannot resolve the immediate issue of these countries' inability to repay their debts, economic growth is still expected to make the developing countries' debt manageable. Indeed, key debtor countries, such as Brazil, Mexico, and Argentina, have generated substantial trade surpluses since 1983. In large part, these surpluses were generated by severe restrictions on imports that reinforced the 1982 recession in the industrialized countries. The sacrifices required to achieve these surpluses may explain the bitterness of the rhetoric directed at the United States and the banks in mid-1984 concerning rising interest rates. Although several major debtor countries have made severe adjustments and cut imports sharply to generate trade surpluses, their debt-servicing burden is so large that their current accounts remain in deficit. The combined current account deficit of developing country debtors dropped from $113 billion in 1981 to $38 billion in 1984 while the seven largest debtors reduced their combined deficit from $40 billion in 1982 to $1.5 billion in 1984.[13]

A projection model developed by William R. Cline in 1983 points to a 3 percent annual economic growth in the industrial countries as a threshold level that will enable debtor countries to increase their exports to the industrial countries, thereby making the developing countries' debt problem manageable. However, this model was built on a number of assumptions, including relatively low interest rates, a depreciating dollar, and relatively low oil prices, changes that did not begin to occur until three years after the model was developed. Changes in interest rates cause major fluctuations in the total amount of the debt-service burden of key developing countries. Interest rate increases during the spring of 1984 prompted sharp outcries by leaders of debtor countries, especially President Raul Alfonsin of Argentina. For example, a 1 percent increase in the London Interbank Offered Rate (LIBOR) adds $900 million to Brazil's current account deficit, while a 1 percent growth in the economies of the industrial countries reduces South Korea's current account deficit by $750 million.[14] Changes in oil prices have a beneficial effect on some debtors and harmful effect on others. Oil-importing countries, such as Brazil, benefit from an oil price drop while an oil exporter, Mexico, for example, is able to generate less revenue.

The volatility of these factors is indicative of the fragility of the reliance on industrial countries' economic growth to pull the debtor countries out of their debt woes. Even though a number of studies confirm a 3 percent annual growth as the key figure, Cline was concerned about whether this economic growth will occur, and if it does, whether it will alleviate the problem. By 1986 the problem has not been remedied by the three years of time projected by the model. Other studies focusing on the need for export growth by the debtor countries also concede the pivotal importance of a favorable world environment and the remedy of time.[15] However, as the president of the BIS has pointedly observed: "Anaemic growth in Western countries would annihilate the hopes of LDC's to expand their exports to any significant degree, and one should start looking for alternative ways to reduce the debt burden of developing nations."[16]

Domestic political pressures for protectionism against imports from developing countries are also a significant threat to a strategy relying on industrial countries' growth as the means of pulling debtor countries out of their predicament. This salient point has been fully recognized by the United States.

> The key to recovery from the debt problem, however, lies in increased exports from the debtor countries. Import restrictions by the developing countries can only accomplish so much in improving their trade balances. Imports have already fallen considerably in high debt countries in the last year, leaving limited room for further cuts. As growth resumes among the debtor countries, they will tend to import more, and will need to export more to pay for the imports. They will not be able to do this if the industrial countries, including the United States, institute new protectionist measures.[17]

Hinging a favorable resolution of the debt problem of developing countries largely on the economic recovery of the industrial countries assumes that the recovery will last and be robust. It leaves debtor countries prey to increasing demands for protectionism in the industrial countries, such as the United States with a 1986 trade deficit of about $150 billion, with about one-third of that amount generated by imports from debtor countries. It also raises a question about the lag time required for an economic recovery in the industrial countries to "trickle down" to the debtor countries and pull them out of their financial difficulties. To date, the overall debt and the debt-service burden of the leading debtor countries continue to account for a substantial portion of their export earnings (see Table 5.1).

TABLE 5.1. Debt to Export Ratios (average of gross external debt at beginning and end of year as percentage of exports of goods and services)

	1982	1984	1985
Argentina	406	473	483
Brazil	339	322	368
Chile	333	402	442
Ecuador	240	260	254
Mexico	299	293	322
Peru	251	330	370
Venezuela	169	177	201
Nigeria	85	165	180
Philippines	270	312	342
Yugoslavia	167	166	160

Source: Peter Montagnon, "Top Bank Warns on Debt Crisis," *The Financial Times*, September 23, 1985, p. 2. Reprinted with permission.

ALTERNATIVE SOLUTIONS

Those who are convinced that there is no arithmetic solution to the international debt problem, even with a robust economic recovery, argue that additional or intermediate measures are necessary, with the essential disagreement revolving around which of the parties will bear what part of the loss. During previous decades, the prescription for one or two countries of relatively small size experiencing financial imbalances was to impose austerity measures. However, with many major debtor countries having such difficulties simultaneously, the imposition of austerity measures may be counterproductive.[18] Critics have charged that austerity programs imposed on many key debtor countries are a prescription for global depression and domestic upheavals.[19]

Most critics of the way the actors in the foreign debt problem have dealt with it thus far begin their assessment with the definition of the problem. They often take the players in the drama to task for refusing to recognize the magnitude of the problem they face. One observer concludes that the key debtor countries took out the loans, but cannot "pay the rent on it and never will be able to. Admission of that fact is the starting point for any solution to the crisis."[20] In the words of another commentator, "Brazilians may be fooling themselves about the costs of a moratorium which would lead to another version of austerity—but they come off as hard realists compared with foreign bankers still clinging to hopes of getting their money back," a point echoed by Henry Kissinger who has argued that it is unrealistic to expect these loans to be repaid or serviced.[21] Accordingly, it may follow that the growing outstanding debt is risky not because certain debtor countries may default since "these countries do not possess the capability and willingness to repay the debt. The debt is risky because political pressures within the United States may prevent the U.S. government from providing the implicit guarantees and explicit real transfers that are necessary in order to continue, support, and service the outstanding debt."[22]

The ad hoc case-by-case approach adopted by creditor governments, international banks, and the IMF has also come under harsh attack. Many critics argue that even if some of the problems confronting debtor countries are unique, most of the underlying causes are similar. They conclude that this constitutes a global debt crisis, not isolated cases of foreign debt difficulties. They point to the growing list of major debtors whose debt-servicing problems can be traced to such factors as a large amount of previous borrowing, the effects of a global recession on their export earnings, and relatively high real rates of interest. Some even claim that the policies of the U.S. government, including a comparatively "strong" dollar and "high" U.S. interest rates caused by a large budget deficit, are at the root of the problem.

Critics of relying on trade as a means of solving the debt crisis usually voice concern about the effects of a downturn in the business cycle and the consequences of a less than 3 percent growth rate in the industrial countries when the foreign debts of major developing countries are growing. Numerous alternative debt relief suggestions to ease the severity of the debt crisis have been made. Many of the suggested alternative solutions are strikingly similar in their design and effect, although a basic difference turns on whether debt relief is necessary or whether providing the debtors with additional time is sufficient. They have been grouped in such general categories as (1) extending current arrangements, (2) smoothing payments and capitalizing interest, (3) linking debt-service payments to export-earnings capabilities, and (4) providing debt relief.[23] A common thread running through several recommendations is to relieve commercial banks of their doubtful loans to developing countries by discounting the loans and transferring them to an international agency. Some of these suggestions have been criticized as short-term alterations not aimed at a fundamental solution. By transferring to international institutions the debt owed to private banks, many of these schemes seek to spread the risk. Of course, critics of this approach argue that the effect of such a transfer is to place the debt burden on taxpayers. In addition, such a transfer is viewed as requiring enormous amounts of capital and not being politically feasible.

These proposals also seek to ease the payment burden of the debtor countries in order to provide them with time to undertake an economic recovery and be able to service the loans. Alternatively, the debt would be rescheduled on more realistic terms, thereby decreasing the likelihood of default. In effect, these transfers would create a secondary market in sovereign loans and increase the flexibility of the parties, although critics maintain that they would require enormous amounts of capital and may not be politically feasible because of popular resistance in industrial countries.

In exchange for their loans, the banks would receive long-term bonds from the agency, backed by the credit of Western governments and tradable on a secondary market. The ultimate objective is to substitute a marketable piece of paper for the banks' doubtful loans,' is the way Morgan Grenfell & Co. chairman G. W. Mackworth-Young summarizes the concept of a world discount house.[24]

Some investment bankers have suggested that the World Bank bear some of the risk of loans extended by commercial banks to developing countries. Felix Rohatyn and G.W. Mackworth-Young, for instance, have argued that the World Bank should purchase part of the private banks' uncollectible loans and issue bonds against them.[25] Rohatyn has proposed that private banks' loans to debtor countries be exchanged for guaranteed, tradable paper, such as long-term, low interest bonds issued by an international financial institution that would, in turn, supply debt relief to these countries. Rohatyn's plan would stretch out $300 billion of short-term loans to 25- to 30-year terms at a 6 percent interest rate or half the then current rate. While debtor countries would save $15 to $20 billion in annual interest payments, banks would lose about one-half of their current cash flow and have to take a write-down of about $150 billion. Despite these bank losses Rohatyn believes the banks' upgrading of their loan portfolios would encourage them to lend more to the debtor countries.[26] Rohatyn has also urged multinational action to cope with the debt crisis and recommended a new Bretton Woods conference to suggest changes in the international monetary system.[27]

Maintaining the liquidity of the banking system is at the core of G.W. Mackworth-Young's plan. He envisages a two-phased operation where, in the first phase, banks would transfer their developing countries' loans to an international financial institution in exchange for noninterest-bearing bonds, thereby relieving them of the burden of funding these loans. During the second phase, these bonds would be converted to guaranteed quadruple-A-rated bonds to be traded in the secondary market. On conversion, however, the banks would mark their securities to market. The major advantage of this two-phased process is the time it provides banks by deferring write-downs until their capital ratios allow it.

The World Bank has been at the heart of numerous proposals involving a transfer of the debt or creation of an insurance mechanism.[28] Richard Weinert has proposed that the World Bank accept up to 80 percent of the private banks' loans to developing countries in exchange for some $150 billion worth of 15- to 25-year bonds. Although there would not be an initial discount, the interest rates on the bonds would be tied to the individual countries' ability to service the debt as determined by an IMF index, but with a maximum to protect debtors and a minimum to insure that banks receive a certain cash flow. Morgan Guaranty's Rimmer de Vries believes the World Bank should be involved in Eurocurrency syndications so it can extend its reach. Société Générale's Yves Laulan wants the World Bank to institute a "cross-default" provision," whereby countries that default on their commercial loans are automatically considered in default with the World Bank as well.[29]

World Bank representatives have been notably unenthusiastic about the particular suggestions for the institution's direct involvement in the global debt problem, although the World Bank has been interested in formulating a role for itself in the debt crisis and has increased its balance-of-payments loans. World Bank President A. W. Clausen's response to the Rohatyn suggestion is that it is none of the World Bank's business. Barend de Vries brands the cross-default suggestion "idiotic" and opposes the World Bank's participation in syndicated loans "that do nothing but throw money down a hole without any conditionality."[30]

Peter Kenen of Princeton University has suggested a modest debt relief proposal focusing on the creation of workable secondary market. His proposed "International Debt Discount Corp" would make a one-time offer to purchase private banks' loans to developing countries at a 10 percent discount. This modest discount would have less drastic effects on banks and taxpayers, but doubts have been raised whether it would provide enough debt relief to the debtor countries. Guttentag and Herring have suggested a six point proposal, urging that loans be marked to market and that banks be encouraged to provide additional loans by distinguishing between old and new loans. Despite shortcomings associated with these proposals, they argue that the markets would accept such valuations.[31]

Norman Bailey, a fomer member of the U.S. National Security Council, has proposed that the banks continue to receive interest on their loans so that they will not have to write down their assets or take a "hit" on their income. However, instead of principal payments, debtor countries could issue an "exchange participation note" that would guarantee the banks a fixed percentage of the debtors' foreign exchange receipts.[32] The banks would, in effect, assume the risk of trade and commodity cycles. In this case, however, a debtor country might have an incentive not to export more than a certain amount because its debt payments would increase with its export earnings.

Doubts about the willingness of Western governments to assume private banks' sovereign risks have stimulated proposals for nationally based rediscounting facilities that would relieve banks of the need to fund these "immobilized assets" and shorten the term of the loan but not transfer the risk.

> Each country's central bank would agree to rediscount its banks' rescheduled, medium-term assets in exchange for a bank commitment to lend the same amount to the LDC's in shorter-term trade finance. If any debtor defaulted, the loans would revert to the bank and be written off; meanwhile, these loans could be carried on the books as contingent liabilities.[33]

Advocates of discounting sovereign debt agree that the ad hoc rescue packages for a number of counties, especially Mexico and Brazil, have bought the key element of time, but at a price. That price for the international banks is taking on additional long-term loans, some argue of lower quality, and funding them with short-term deposits. Furthermore, these critics argue that the international system requires more than ad hoc rescue packages, given that over 25 countries with debts in excess of 40 percent of total developing country debt are struggling to reschedule their debt obligations.[34] The cost to the banks of such discounting has been estimated at 3 percent of annual earnings representing a 50 percent reduction of current cash flows attributable to those loans. A mandatory write-down of the loans to reflect the reduced cash flow has been estimated to cost $50 billion.

Proponents of such an official disount mechanism argue that the banks would be the primary beneficiaries of the device. "They would at once upgrade their portfolios and free up their balance sheets for new loans at home and abroad."[35] Some advocates of discounting schemes argue that commercial banks cannot fulfill the role of balance-of-payments financing and carry the burden of developing countries' adjustment programs. Balance-of-payments financing is a relatively new role borne by private banks during the 1970s—a role that had, until that time, belonged to the international financial agencies, to whom, argue these critics, it should revert. Private banks would then return to their traditional roles of supplying self-liquidating trade credit and project financing.

A major drawback to a discounting scheme is that the loans would be purchased at below face value, thereby requiring the banks to write off the losses and have a significant negative impact on their capital ratios. The high visibility accompanying such an event would also lead shareholders and depositors to shun such banks, thereby raising their funding costs. Since numerous bankers maintain that the current debt problem is a "temporary liquidity problem," they are opposed to such schemes which they often scorn as academic. Nonetheless, many bankers have nagging doubts about the quality of their loans to key debtor countries and believe that a more fundamental solution may well be needed.

Proposals have also been made that debtor countries sell some of their assets to their creditors or engage in debt-for-equity swaps. "For those countries with large endowments of natural resources or profitable state-owned enterprises, this is certainly an option worth considering."[36] This may be a worthwhile option if it would demonstrate the debtors' desire to take action and involve the industrialized countries in the LDC debt problem. However, implementing such an alternative by, for instance, having Brazil pay off its loans by offering lender banks stock in state-owned enterprises may not be particularly attractive for either party. The image of the government may be eroded because Brazilians do not favor handing over control of national assets. Bankers are unlikely to be any happier owing shares of a state company rather than loans. As one expert notes, "Most of the companies are so unprofitable that instead of a nonperforming loan, the banks would be stuck with another nonperforming asset."[37] Nonetheless, Mexico has reportedly proposed allowing foreign banks to exchange their loans to state-owned firms for partial ownership of such enterprises, despite the likely political criticism such a plan may generate.[38] Several private Mexican firms have reportedly negotiated equity transfers to their creditors.

The alternative of a substantial grace period on interest payments or a form of interest rate subsidies is not viewed with favor by the banks, which, from their perspective, have recently lowered the interest rate spreads to what they feel is the limit and worry about this precedent as much as about a moratorium. Nevertheless, several recent reschedulings, especially, for example, those with Mexico and Brazil, have included long grace periods, reduced interest rate spreads, and maturities of up to 15 years. Nor are bankers enthusiastic about proposals calling for half of the debtor countries' repayment to be in local currency, rather than dollars, proposals that would also require substantial changes in the way banking regulators would treat such payments.

A proposal originally made by Tony Solomon, former president of the Federal Reserve Bank of New York, is to cap the interest rate of loans to debtor countries by allowing the borrower to extend the maturity of the loan when the interest rate rises above a specified level such that the interest is converted into principal to be paid later. Indeed, the World Bank has made such a loan.

Martin Feldstein modified the interest rate cap proposal by suggesting that multi-year reschedulings keep interest costs constant even if interest rates rise by automatically triggering more loans to debtor countries to cover additional interest costs. The debtor countries' owed principal would increase, but the annual interest cost would remain constant. Since the banks would recover lost interest through increases in the principal amount, David Rockefeller endorsed this approach as an attractive way for banks to be encouraged to keep lending to debtor countries.[39] "Capping" interest rates and capitalizing interest payments may offer advantages to the banks, debtors, and bank regulators. Bank earnings may not be affected, bank regulators may find this an appropriate and flexible approach, and the debtors will have a constant payment obligation. Thus far, however, bank regulators have not received the "capping" proposals with enthusiasm.

Yet another alternative (and indeed one of the few that addresses the question about how to proceed with future lending) suggested by Richard Dale of Brookings Institution, is to provide the IMF with the authority to guarantee new bank loans in exchange for a fee. The Trilateral Commission proposes, as one alternative, providing a form of insurance or guarantee to cover a portion of the risk or banks' portfolios, or having debtor countries issue securities, with or without a guarantee.[40]

Creation of a government-guaranteed secondary market in developing country loans is unlikely to be seriously considered unless defaults seem imminent. The U.S. government has stated its opposition to guaranteeing private bank loans to debtor countries.[41] Taxpayers would bear a significant burden if such a guarantee scheme is implemented. The U.S. Treasury Department has refused to explore alternative solutions arguing that it is "not in the business of getting the

American taxpayer to bail out either the debtor countries or the creditor banks."[42] International financial institutions have been unenthusiastic about becoming a safety net or lenders of last resort. Banks would also bear a large cost, a major reason banks are not interested in such schemes. Yet banks would likely reconsider their position if they found themselves with nonperforming loans on their books for a prolonged period. There may be a time when massive debt relief may be viewed as necessary and a discount scheme may be seen as attractive. As one banker has observed, "If we thought we weren't going to be repaid, we would see lots more merit in the scheme."[43]

Others have come out in opposition to discounting schemes that would transfer private banks' existing sovereign risks to governments on the grounds that it would remove market discipline. Some argue that such schemes fail to take account of the unique attributes of these debtor countries.[44] Others claim that banks and countries should be kept at risk in order to insure the health and discipline of international banking. A few observers even go so far as to suggest that building a safety net might be detrimental because it might encourage debtor countries to renege once they realize that the banks will not be harmed by such a move.[45]

Bankers argue that they have renegotiated the debts of developing countries with an eye to making repayment schedules fit each country's ability to repay, as well as providing additional credit to stimulate their economies and generate additional exports. However, if private banks were forced to absorb losses on discounted assets, they would not appear to be leading candidates to provide new loans, although Rohatyn seems to believe the banks would continue to lend. In the words of one international banker, "If you sell off part of your portfolio at a discount, would *you* turn around and lend 100 cents on the dollar to the same country?"[46]

The case-by-case ad hoc response to the current debt problem has been characterized as damage control and those making this case argue that action is needed now because it will be too late to do so during a future crisis. For example, Leland S. Prussia, chairman of Bank of America Corp., argues that the Third World debt crisis is a "fundamental structural problem requiring long-term solutions," not a short-term liquidity problem.[47] He has suggested three steps to achieve growth in debtor countries and to provide an incentive for creditors to continue lending. First, multi-year reschedulings; second, capping the total amount of debtors' annual payments; and third, encouraging new trade financing through refinancing by international organizations. Robert V. Roosa, former undersecretary of the Treasury and now a partner at Brown Brothers Harriman, looks to the Chrysler and Lockheed "bailout" models as a means of restoring debtor country viability.[48] The major elements of Mr. Roosa's plan are:

1. The initiation of a comprehensive program for the private and public sectors of LDCs that would combine "corrective retrenchment with structural rehabilitation";

2. Providing the borrowers with a grace period of several years for payment of principal with a schedule for such payments, linked to future currency earnings, to
   be agreed upon at the end of the grace period;
3. Reduction of the spread over LIBOR on new or rescheduled loans, contingent on
   the borrower's success in meeting its IMF criteria and other conditions;
4. Participation by the World Bank in a long-term reconstruction program and
   cofinancing arrangements with commercial banks; and
5. Infusion of additional short- and medium-term loans from the IMF, commercial
   banks, and other sources to be disbursed in relation to a debtor country's movement toward agreed-upon goals.[49]

Although he agrees that banks may balk at the idea of undertaking the measures in order to maintain the value of their outstanding loans by taking some
losses while putting in additional funds into debtor countries, Roosa argues that
the major advantage of his plan is its quick implementation since no new institutions would have to be created. In addition, he is convinced that action to reduce the debtor countries' burden has to be taken as soon as possible, that playing a continuous shell game whereby banks make loans so that debtor countries
can pay them the interest serves little purpose, and that banks must come to the
realization that their self-interest is not served by driving these countries to a point
where they can no longer service their debts.

Some would agree with Roosa's assessment that even if the key to the debt
crisis lies in buying time for the growth of international trade to take hold, the
key question that remains unanswered is what measures will be taken during the
intervening period. Many of those who argue that no fundamental changes are
needed do, however, agree that greater supervision by bank regulatory agencies,
including specific measures to coordinate and disseminate lending information
so that the exposure is readily apparent, can contribute to greater prudence in
international lending activities.

Even Fidel Castro has entered the field of international finance by arguing
that the Latin debt is unpayable as structured and proposing that the United States
and other industrialized countries pay the international banks the approximately
$360 billion owed by Latin America.[50] Coming on the heels of a plea for debt
assistance from heads of many Latin states to the heads of industrialized countries meeting at the Bonn economic summit in 1985, Castro's proposal has stirred
interest, even if his motives are suspect.

Those who view the debt problem in a wider political context argue that U.S.
relations with Latin America must not be dominated by periodic concerns about
the collection of interest payments, especially as the United States seeks to foster democratic regimes in the region.[51] Pointing to the dangers inherent in the
continuation of a policy that breeds frustration after considerable sacrifice by Latin
American states, Kissinger argues that new measures should be adopted in order to instill hope and improve the relationship between the United States and
key Latin debtors. In particular, he combines several suggestions made by others

for "capping" interest rates, providing the debtors with more time, as well as establishing a Western Hemisphere Development Institution to raise funds in the international capital markets to be lent to the debtors at a low and fixed interest rate.[52]

Although some bankers maintain that their loans to key debtor countries are worth 100 percent of face value, some activity with respect to such loans belies that contention. Some banks have reexamined their loan portfolios and conducted some loan swaps to reduce their exposure, with some developing countries' loans discounted 50 percent. Citibank negotiated a $900 million insurance policy with Cigna on a package of its foreign loans, a policy subsequently canceled by Cigna.[53] Even though the idea of transferring some of this bank exposure to the insurance industry may have been appealing, the insurance industry has not sought such additional policies, perhaps because the value of Cigna stock dropped with the announcement of the Citibank deal which was eventually terminated.

Although the creation of a private secondary market in developing countries' outstanding loans is unlikely to become a significant part of a possible discounting solution to the debt problem, such a market has developed. For example, EU-RINAM (European InterAmerican Finance Corp.) has been dealing in 5 to 25 percent discounted restructured Latin American assets in the $100 to $200 million range. Reacting to their problem loans to Latin American countries, commercial banks have begun to swap loans "that make them extremely uncomfortable for loans that make them a little less uncomfortable."[54] Some Middle Eastern and European banks have put their entire Latin American loan portfolio up for swap.[55]

Bankers Trust has swapped about a dozen of its loans to reduce its exposure to Brazil. This has raised eyebrows because Bankers Trust is a member of the advisory committee that was engaged in putting together a $6.5 billion financial package for Brazil. A $290 million swap between Bankers Trust and Banco Real, a private Brazilian bank experiencing difficulties obtaining foreign deposits, is illustrative. "If Mexican paper is unpalatable to U.S. banks, Brazilian paper seems practically poisonous."[56] In exchange for Banco Real's loans to Mexico, Bankers Trust transferred cash and loans to Brazil. Bankers Trust was worried that its Brazilian loans were close to becoming nonperforming and that U.S. bank regulatory agencies would require it to reserve against these loans which would be charged against earnings. At the time, it viewed Mexican loans as more likely to be paid.

Some bankers criticize those banks engaging in Brazilian loan swaps because they believe the priority should be to help the borrowing countries overcome a crisis. They argue that it makes it harder to convince regional banks to make additional loans when an advisory committee member is engaging in such swaps. Nonetheless, most observers doubt this type of swap activity will be of major financial significance, even as some banks seek to continue reducing their exposure.

CONCLUSION

In assessing the unfolding of the foreign debt problem, some analysts choose to place the bulk of the blame on what they regard as imprudent lending by international banks, while others lay the blame on the policies of the debtor countries. These assessments may be opposite sides of the same coin, since lenders and borrowers are in a reciprocal relationship. However, there is a consensus that external factors exacerbated the problem, namely that "at the very time when debt service burdens were escalating, the developing countries' sources of hard currency earnings were evaporating."[57] For example, the dramatic rise of interest rates combined with an escalating debt burden caused the interest payments of Mexico, Brazil, and Argentina to quadruple between 1978 and 1981.[58]

Erroneous assumptions contributed to flawed actions taken by each of the parties in the debt drama and blame for the current difficulties can be widely distributed. Assigning blame may be useful in avoiding future mistakes or even in allocating losses each of the parties might have to take if certain scenarios occur. International banks were attracted by the opportunities and growth potential in certain developing countries and, along with the borrowers, failed to take seriously the possibility that their most fundamental assumptions with respect to the environmental risks could change dramatically and place both parties in a vulnerable position.

Creditor governments and their bank regulatory authorities failed to provide clear warnings or establish adequate safeguards with respect to the risks associated with the dramatic rise in international lending. During the 1970s they seemed to encourage the process of "petrodollar recycling." Although issuing warnings on occasion about the exposure and concentration of such lending, creditor governments and their regulators were ambivalent about these developments. Furthermore, with the advent of the Mexican crisis of August 1982, they acted to ensure that lending from the banks to the major debtor countries would continue.

Critics argue that the regulators chose to ignore the problem of increased bank exposure and concentration and charge that these actions were simply not prudent. In any event, during 1984 the U.S. regulators prodded the major U.S. banks to begin to take a "hit" on earnings as the loans to Argentina began to be classified as nonperforming. This action caused Manufacturers Hanover, Argentina's largest lender, to suffer a $21.4 million cut in its 1984 second quarter earnings.[59]

Allocation of blame provides only limited guidance about how to proceed in assuring a favorable outcome to the debt problem afflicting the international financial system. The parties involved in the current debt problem have cooperated to provide time for economic growth to take root. Each of the parties has sought to use the available time to implement measures to alleviate the pressures of global debt. Debtor countries have used the intervening period to make harsh, but necessary, adjustments in their domestic policies and import demands.

The nervous reaction of international banks and their loan cutbacks exacerbated the difficulties of major debtor countries seeking to service their previous loan obligations. Combined with the effects of the global recession, a sharp increase in real interest rates and a rise in the value of the dollar in which most of their loans were denominated, the impact on major debtor countries has caused significant declines in their economic activity.[60]

Additional lending to debtor countries by creditor governments, the IMF, the BIS, and many international banks has been based on a fundamental assumption, namely that the debtor countries are experiencing temporary liquidity difficulties. Even though major debtor countries require significant increases in capital flows to stimulate growth and development, commercial banks have been chastened by their recent experiences and are reluctant to increase their exposure unless absolutely necessary. However, if debtor countries conclude that their plight is worsening, their debt repayments are getting increasingly onerous, and their exports earnings are insufficient to repay their interest payments, they may have little incentive to continue servicing their foreign debt obligations. If voluntary,'' may well be in the self-interest of banks as they come face to face with ger a repudiation.

Banks have used the intervening time to reschedule outstanding loans to debtor countries. Initially, the exchanges between the banks and their country borrowers were characterized as a "dialogue of the deaf" as banks sought a high rate of return while the debtor countries sought better terms. Nevertheless, the sums rescheduled in 1983–1984, approaching about $80 billion, are staggering, especially in comparison with those of the mid-1970s. Critics argue that such reschedulings merely postpone the problem, especially in light of the recent 1985–1986 $100 billion reschedulings for Mexico and Brazil. Moreover, additional time has also provided these banks with the opportunity to provision or reserve for such loans, an act that some banks have taken either voluntarily or at the insistence of bank regulators in the case of several countries. Indeed, some argue that the international banks should be reserving against loans to the leading debtor countries because the current situation is unsustainable and that such countries will cease making their debt payments by the end of the decade.

> Private banks must play a crucial role in the restructuring effort. After all they have billions of dollars at stake. They must offer LDC's some time. Actually the banks need the time themselves: they have their own balance sheets to clean up. Patience and a lot of discipline are necessary. We are all in the same boat and there is no place for free-riders here. It may seem somewhat counterintuitive to ask banks to throw good money after bad, so to say. But there is no other way. We are in a situation where the social costs of not acting far exceed the private costs.[61]

Banks are cognizant of the constraint imposed by the lender's dilemma they face. "The banking community realizes that the future prospects of most major debtor countries are bright, and that it would be a serious mistake to jeopardize the soundness of the large volume of existing loans by refusing to make relatively small additional loans."[62] In short, continued lending, even if "involuntary," may well be in the self-interest of banks as they come face to face with the lender's dilemma: if they stop lending the value of their outstanding loans would be eroded, but if they continue to lend they could be pouring in good money after bad. Many banks have responded to this constraint by curtailing the growth of their international exposure while seeking greater growth opportunites in other financial sectors of their domestic markets, thereby, over time, lowering the percentage of their international loans in relation to their total assets.

However, the strategy of providing additional resources based on the diagnosis that the world is facing a temporary liquidity crisis requires a degree of discipline to assure that major banks continue their lending and that shortsighted self-interest does not motivate individual banks to withdraw. Even though a number of banks have sought to swap the debts of some of the leading developing countries, some have ridiculed the effort, comparing it to "rearranging the deck chairs on the Titanic."[63]

In light of their intertwined interests, it would appear that debtor countries should be motivated not to repudiate their loans, while banks not declare these debtors in default or withdraw from international lending. This convergence of interests may be fragile as banks face a "lending trap" and the debtor countries confront a "debt trap."[64] Creditor countries and international banks had hoped that the 1985 Mexican developments would serve as the model for the path out of the current debt problem. Mexico's creditors reduced their new loans to Mexico but agreed to lower their interest rate and fees as a reward for Mexico's austerity measures and economic progress. This reduces the increase in the banks' exposure and may increase the likelihood of repayment. Indeed, the multi-year rescheduling for Mexico, a key ingredient of the Mexican model, was a key in the strategy deployed by the major banks to defuse the debt crisis. However, Mexico's subsequent problems reinforced the nervousness of the international financial community.

If the economic recovery is not sufficient to pull the major debtor countries out of their current debt predicament or a future recession sets in, other measures, including the various alternative solutions, such as discounting and transfer schemes, may be strongly advocated once again. In light of the numerous alternative solutions offered as a remedy to the global debt problem, it is unlikely that additional proposals appear to be the most pressing need, especially since the U.S. Treasury Department has criticized and rejected calls "to do something" about the debt crisis through an across-the-board or comprehensive solution by arguing that no such solution exists.[65]

In June 1985, Preston Martin, the then vice-chairman of the Federal Reserve Bank, called for an examination of innovative proposals for dealing with the international debt problem and highlighted differences of opinion with respect to the success of the U.S. government's debt strategy. Coming at a time when Federal Reserve Chairman Volcker was engaged in international negotiations to endorse the adequacy of the current case-by-case approach, Preston Martin's remarks were sharply criticized by Volcker. Whether Martin's call for reexamination of these proposals was advanced in the nature of a contingency plan or a trial balloon was unclear, but his comments may have left the impression that a change in the U.S. debt strategy was forthcoming and that there was an "easier way" out of the debt crisis. Chairman Volcker issued the following statement:

> I find his [Mr. Martin's] reported comments incomprehensible, and unfortunately and unrealistically suggesting that there are unorthodox approaches to deal with the international debt problem. What is hopeful and promising is that so many countries are coming to grips with necessary and difficult adjustment efforts. One example is the highly promising effort currently under way in Argentina.[66]

The U.S. Department of the Treasury argued in 1983 that the global debt problem can be divided into three phases: a crisis atmosphere over liquidity, an effort by developed and developing countries to grapple with the steps needed to improve the world economy, and an orderly resolution of the debt problems. According to the Treasury's analysis, the world community is entering the third phase, although resolution of the financial problems of the debtor countries is "at least a couple of years away."[67] The American Society suggests that a series of measures may be needed.[68] Pointing to the negotiations by Mexico for multi-year rescheduling, the Department of the Treasury also argues that the prevailing pessimism over the debt problem is unwarranted because progress is being made. The marked decline in the offering of alternative proposals may reflect an improving environment. Others, however, do not foresee a resolution of these problems until the end of the 1980s, if then. Indeed, many experts doubt that the creditworthiness of many key debtor countries will be established in the foreseeable future or that voluntary lending by major banks will be forthcoming. "The debt problem will not just go away. It will stay with us for quite some time yet. Austerity and growth need time to take effect. . . . During this period it is vital that public and private financial institutions cooperate to [sic] the general effort."[69]

Many critics claim that the time provided by the recent ad hoc arrangements has not been utilized effectively. Characterizing the movements of the actors in the debt drama as little more than muddling through the evolving plot, they argue that this foreign debt burden is growing and that the seeds of a larger future debt crisis are being planted as reflected by the maturity bunching and ever-increasing debt figures expected in the 1987–88 period and beyond. Even those advocates of buying time realize its limitations and the need for additional action.

> We certainly are not over the hill yet with the debt problem, but...the danger of an uncontrollable catastrophe is considerably less today than it was twelve months ago. We have won some time, and we must now use it to set down a strategy that will pave the way for a long-run solution. That this solution cannot consist in indefinitely extending new credits to developing nations should be clear, just as the flow of money cannot be suddenly interrupted. Equally obvious is the fact that the strategy must deal with questions that extend well beyond financing matters.[70]

A number of critics have argued that policymakers must adopt measures that go "beyond the quick fix."[71] These assessments question a number of features in the current approach to the debt problem, particularly how long major debtor countries can continue their austerity programs, how long the IMF can continue its disciplinary role, the implications arising from and future implications of the enormous reschedulings, and the strains on bank regulators who must balance the need of prudent and sound banking practices with major debtor countries' need for additional financing. Some bankers and country risk analysts are also reflecting their frustrations. A bank field representative complains that "back home they want to hear that Brazil is doing well. They want to hear that the IMF policies are working, that Brazil is over the worst and so on because the alternative would mean addressing more serious issues."[72] Such complaints have been echoed by banks' country risk analysts who feel that insufficient attention is being given to their assessments. "I keep trying to bang it into their heads that social tensions are building up in Mexico, but it's enough for them that Mexico's interest payments are up to date."[73]

By 1985, as Third World debt approached $1 trillion, many bankers were relieved that dire predictions regarding the debt crisis had not been realized. Some even went so far as to proclaim that the debt bomb had been "defused" and that the crisis was "all but over."[74] Indeed, not only had Mexico and Brazil performed better than had been anticipated, but Argentina had reached agreement with the IMF and had repaid a substantial portion of its interest arrears, thereby allowing many banks to include these amounts in their earnings for 1984. These developments may have lulled bankers into complacency at a time when numerous debt problems were lurking on the horizon, especially as negotiations with key debtors became strained, other countries joined the growing list of debtors, and banking regulators insisted on larger loan loss reserves and certain write-offs. As Brazil and Argentina fell out of compliance with their IMF programs, their inability to obtain credit from the IMF also delayed their commercial bank loans. Since U.S. bank regulators had declared Argentine loans substandard in the past, commercial banks were anxious about the consequences of such possible measures. Considered a model debtor since 1982, Mexico's falling out of compliance with its IMF program prompted one international observer to note: "I don't know if you can call Mexico's problems with the IMF a disaster, but it is disquieting."[75] Others were concerned about the inadequate rescheduling packages being provided to smaller debtor countries, particularly several Latin American as well as Central American and African states, which are also experiencing severe political strains.[76] In short, the debt crisis may be "in remission at best."[77]

With increasing criticism mounting over the continued utility of the case-by-case approach and mounting fear that debtor countries would adopt unilateral measures of potential harm to all the parties involved in the debt problem, there were renewed calls for the United States to take a bold initiative on the debt crisis. For example, Morgan Guaranty warned that the measures taken since 1982 had not fulfilled their intended purpose. With a U.S. economic slowdown and a drop of exports by the leading debtors, Morgan Guaranty concluded that economic growth in the industrial countries has to be stimulated, interest rates must be lowered, the commercial banks have to be persuaded to increase their lending to the debtors, and the multilateral financial institutions—such as the World Bank through its long-term structured adjustment loans, cofinancing, issuance of partial guarantees for commercial bank loans, and a loan-sale program—must increase their lending.[78]

The debtor countries' frustration, impatience and "adjustment fatigue" have prompted concern within the U.S. government regarding their financial and political problems, particularly those confronting Latin American states. There is also concern that these debtor countries may adopt a more confrontational stance. An Inter-American Development Bank study has sharply criticized IMF measures as short-term and inadequate. It suggests that there is no support for the continued transfer of resources from the region even under conditions of global trade growth. The conclusion emphasizes the need to lay the foundation for long-term growth.[79]

Unveiled at the 1985 IMF-World Bank annual meetings, the U.S. government's most recent debt initiative, known as the Baker Plan, has its focus on the World Bank, growth, and increased financing. It has been cast as emphasizing the need for more structural adjustment—such as encouraging foreign direct investment, decreasing government intervention in the markets, and lessening the reliance on public sector entities—by debtor countries, long-term World Bank loans to Latin America as a means of easing the debt burden, and increased commercial bank lending, and not as an abandonment of the U.S. Treasury's case-by-case approach. In a change of U.S. emphasis, the World Bank's participation in ameliorating the debt crisis would also include guarantees for commercial bank loans as a means of encouraging their agreement to provide additional new capital. In addition, the Inter-American Development Bank as well as the other regional development banks would have a larger role in encouraging more foreign investment.[80]

Although several financial leaders have lauded the U.S. initiative, some representatives of debtor countries have greeted it with skepticism and criticized it as too little, too late. Yet the willingness of the U.S. government to express its concern, stake out a leadership role, and suggest a more activist approach, as opposed to leaving the issue to be resolved between the debtor countries and their creditor banks, may signal a turning point in the political context of the debt problem. Although the 1985 debt initiative has been described as a shift from an emphasis on austerity to one of growth, the previous strategy also relied on growth. Nonetheless, critics argue growth thus far has been disappointing and current forecasts do not seem to provide a basis for optimism.

There have been numerous assessments regarding those elements necessary to reestablish confidence. Although there are critics who suggest that many Latin American states will refuse to service their debts even with global economic growth, the U.S. debt initiative focuses on economic growth as the means to achieve confidence. Nevertheless, even a variety of key assumptions, such as 3 percent growth by industrialized countries, low interest rates, a fall in the value of the dollar, and declining oil prices, yield a gap of a magnitude that can only be financed by international commercial banks. Although debtor countries must adopt adjustment measures to reestablish confidence and generate foreign invest-ment, their access to additional financing, both public and private, seems to hinge on their satisfactory economic performance. However, the weariness of a three year IMF-centered adjustment process has reinforced the tension facing commer-cial banks between concern for their outstanding loans and desire to curtail their exposure.

The international commercial banks have not resumed voluntary lending nor increased their exposure because, they argue, they are trying to reestablish their soundness and safety. Yet without the agreement of commerical banks to increase their exposure to the major debtor countries, it is unclear how the pressure on these countries will be eased or what incentives they will have to maintain ad-justment programs. International commercial banks remain cautious about in-creasing their exposure to debtor countries, and it remains unclear whether they will be willing to do so.

Accordingly, there have been calls for altering U.S. regulatory criteria by, for example, permitting the capitalization of interest. With new lending, com-mercial banks could, arguably, improve the value of their outstanding loans, al-though many banks might choose not to increase their exposure since they view themselves as overexposed already. Whether such "free riders" could be coerced into providing additional funds remains unclear, especially since there are fears among some officals that the U.S. government could be held accountable if such loans were declared a loss at a later date.[81] U.S. Secretary of the Treasury James Baker has noted the difficulty of convincing these commercial banks to increase their lending to the debtor countries by some $20 billion during the 1986–1988 period by suggesting that he has "no intention of twisting arms" and expects these banks to do so because of their stake in the process.[82]

A major goal of the Baker Plan is to restore the creditworthiness of debtor countries and reverse the trend that has resulted in the debtor countries becoming net capital exporters, a paradoxical and untenable situation. Indeed, in 1985 the debtor nations paid $22 billion more to their creditors than they obtained in new loans. Furthermore, the funds lent by the banks to the debtor countries have been characterized as ''round tripping,'' that is, a process whereby the banks lend money to the countries that proceed to use part or all of it to pay the interest on their outstanding loans. These funds are added to the prior obligation and the debt burden to be served by the countries continues to swell.[83]

Many critics argue that the current debt mechanisms foster an illusion and that there is no arithmetic solution to the debt crisis even with reschedulings and the Baker Plan's recipe for economic growth.[84] The plan itself has been criticized for not constituting a plan and for being utopian.[85] Others even argue that the present approach is only making matters worse.[86] Despite such assessments, certain improvements in the international economic environment, especially the decline in real interest rates, the fall in the value of the dollar, and continued growth in the industrial countries, have improved the prospects of certain debtors. However, in addition to the strains posed by the decline in the price of oil for such debtors as Mexico and Venezuela, the major obstacles facing the Baker Plan appear to be the lack of enthusiasm by the banks and the perception that the plan lacks an operational dimension.

In a June 29, 1986 speech, Senator Bill Bradley voiced his concerns about the shrinkage of United States exports to Latin America and the loss of United States employment as a result of the debt problem.[87] He attacked the Baker Plan as calling for new loans and more debt rather than interest rate and debt relief. By calling for debt relief, the Bradley Plan, as the speech has come to be known, is being viewed as an alternative to the Baker Plan, despite arguments that the Bradley Plan itself is flawed. The Bradley Plan builds on the linkage between debt relief and trade expansion. It seeks to encourage economic reforms by debtor countries through forgiveness of existing loans and reducing interest rates, rather than relying on new lending as provided by the Baker Plan. The debt relief goals for eligible countries set forth in the Bradley Plan for trade relief packages are: (1) an interest rate reduction of 3 percent for one year on outstanding loans; (2) a 3 percent writedown and forgiveness of principal on outstanding loans; and (3) new multilateral project and structural adjustment loans totalling $3 billion.

Certain key debtor nations have also not shown a willingness to participate. Apparently they may be reluctant to move their economies toward free markets through significant domestic economic reforms, a condition required by the Baker Plan.[88] In addition, certain countries are sensitive to appearing to serve as a test case for a U.S. plan and being subservient to U.S. interests.

The commercial banks have endorsed the Baker Plan but to date no funds have been forthcoming, although the 1986 Mexican financing package may be viewed as the first Baker Plan case. Indeed, the only element implemented thus far is $3 billion IMF facility to assist growth-oriented economic programs in extremely depressed countries, such as sub-Saharan Africa.[89] Both the U.S. Treasury and the IMF have warned commercial banks that they cannot wait until the debtor countries improve their economic performance before lending them new funds because such countries require the net new lending to achieve these improvements. Nevertheless, the banks have been chastened by their recent international experience and are reluctant to lend. In short, both the lenders and debtors are suffering from "debt fatigue," the borrowers are tired of austerity while the creditors are fearful of increasing their exposure.[90]

The U.S. Treasury has even been sensitive to criticism from banks that the policy of encouraging net new lending is often neutralized by more stringent regulatory controls. Yet the U.S. Treasury has rejected calls by banks for "more details" on the U.S. debt initiative prior to committing new funds or for regulatory concessions from the U.S. government. "What we need instead is for the commercial banks to pitch in and do their share, thereby helping both the debtor countries and the international financial institutions to move the process forward, a process . . . vital to the interests of the banks themselves."[91]

Although the Baker Plan has been described as a program "scrambling to engineer a 'success,' " the initiative has succeeded in launching a new process and preempting demands for more radical approaches.[92] It remains to be seen whether the critics are correct in maintaining that it is only a matter of time before one of the debt relief alternatives must be implemented. Clearly, however, the Baker Plan's appeal for more cooperation among debtors and creditors to avoid potentially disruptive confrontations requires that the funds promised be forthcoming. Having raised expectations significantly, the Baker Plan has formidable obstacles to overcome in order to fulfill them.[93]

The unfolding of future events will determine which school of thought—the optimists or the pessimists—is correct in its assessments. Most observers still believe that the likelihood is high that the players in the current debt drama will manage to muddle through yet another financial storm. In short, the probability of a massive loan repudiation or default is low, even if the consequences would be severe. Whether this merely postpones the problem and yields ever-larger future foreign debt crises is left unanswered. The vulnerability of bankers and creditor governments as a result of debtor countries' burden has been compared to Pascal's wager—"betting one's soul against an event which combines a catastrophic outcome with a low probability of occurrence."[94] Pascal argued that a reasonable person would not make such a bet, but Congress noted its concern with the type of betting undertaken by many international banks. "A banking system that is constantly on the brink of disaster and subject to never-ending threats of default does not inspire confidence."[95] Confidence remains the core of the country creditworthiness issue as key debtors seek to restore growth and development. Whether creditworthiness can be restored remains a critical unknown. At a minimum, patience, time, and cooperation are essential to allow each of the parties to adopt measures to improve the situation.

NOTES

1. Sally A. Shelton and Richard Nuccio, "The Next Latin Debt Crisis," The New York *Times*, January 22, 1984.

2. Donald T. Regan, "IMF Resources, World Financial Stability, and U.S. Interests," statement before the Senate Committee on Foreign Relations, Washington, D.C., February 23, 1983.

3. Alfred J. Watkins, *Till Debt Do Us Part* (Washington, D.C.: Roosevelt Center for American Policy Studies, 1986).

4. *The World Bank Annual Report 1983,* p. 34.

5. For example, see Robert D. Muldoon, "Rethinking the Ground Rules for an Open World Economy," *Foreign Affairs,* Summer 1983, p. 1089.

6. Anthony Solomon, "Toward a More Resilient International Financial System," *Federal Reserve Bank of New York Quarterly Review,* Autumn 1983, p. 1.

7. Hobart Rowen, "IMF Director Questions Baker Plan's Formula," The Washington *Post,* March 20, 1986.

8. A. David Knox, "Resuming Growth in Latin America," *Finance and Development,* September 1985.

9. Kenneth W. Dam as quoted in Clyde H. Farnsworth, "IMF Approving $20 Billion Aid for Argentina," New York *Times,* December 29, 1984.

10. Fritz Leutwiler, "International Indebtedness and World Trade," International Monetary and Trade Conference, Philadelphia, Pa., December 4, 1983. Also see William E. Brock, "Trade and Debt: The Vital Linkage," *Foreign Affairs,* Summer 1984, p. 1037.

11. Leutwiler, op. cit., p. 6.

12. *Newsweek,* "Barter: A Way to Defuse the Debt Bomb?" April 15, 1985, p. 17.

13. *World Economic Outlook,* Washington, D.C.: International Monetary Fund, April 1985.

14. *Euromoney,* "Capitalism Under Stress," October 1983, p. 64.

15. William R. Cline, *International Debt and the Stability of the World Economy* (Washington, D.C.: Institute for International Economics, 1983); John Calverly, *Restoring Creditworthiness* (London: The Amex Bank Review Special Papers, January 1984); Ronald Leven and David L. Roberts, "Latin America's Prospects for Recovery," *Federal Reserve Bank of New York Quarterly Review,* Autumn 1983.

16. Leutwiler, op. cit., p. 8.

17. *Economic Report of the President 1983,* Washington, D.C.: USGPO, 1983.

18. Carlos Langoni, remarks before CATO Institute Conference, "World Debt and the Monetary Order," Washington, D.C.: January 21, 1984.

19. John Eisendrath, "How the IMF Makes the World Safe for Depression," *The Washington Monthly,* February 1983; *Euromoney,* "The IMF vs. the People," October 1983, p. 90.

20. Norman Gall, "Games Bankers Play," *Forbes,* December 5, 1983, p. 186.

21. Edward Boyer, "Why Lenders Should Still Be Scared," *Fortune,* December 12, 1983, p. 128.

22. Tamir Agmon, *Political Economy and Risk in World Financial Markets* (Lexington, Massachusetts: Lexington Books, 1985).

23. Fred Bergsten, William R. Cline, and John Williamson, *Bank Lending to Developing Countries: The Policy Alternatives* (Washington, D.C.: Institute for International Economics, April 1985).

24. Linda Sandler, "Is Discounting Sovereign Debt the Way Out," *Institutional Investor,* July 1983, p. 73.

25. See *Institutional Investor,* July 1983 (entire issue), and also Andrew Marton, "Can the World Bank Survive the LDC Debt Crisis," *Institutional Investor,* September 1983, p. 197.

26. Sandler, op. cit., p. 76.

27. Felix G. Rohatyn, "How to Defuse the World's Financial Time Bomb," *Business Week,* December 16, 1985.

28. Henry C. Wallich, *Insurance of Bank Lending to Developing Countries* (New York: Group of Thirty, 1984).

29. Marton, op. cit., p. 197.

30. As quoted in ibid.

31. Jack M. Guttentag and Richard J. Herring, *The Current Crisis in International Lending* (Washington, D.C.: The Brookings Institution, 1985).

32. Norman A. Bailey, R. David Luft, and Roger W. Robinson, Jr., "Exchange Participation Notes: An Approach to the International Financial Crisis," Thibaut de Saint Phalle, (ed.), *The International Financial Crisis: An Opportunity for Constructive Action* (Washington, D.C.: Georgetown University, 1983), p. 27.

33. Proposal by Peter Leslie of Barclays Bank International in Linda Sandler, "Is Discounting Sovereign Debt the Way Out," *Institutional Investor,* July 1983, p. 73.

34. Ibid.

35. Ibid., p. 74.

36. Leutwiler, op. cit., p. 8.

37. Edward Boyer, "Why Lenders Should Still Be Scared," *Fortune,* December 12, 1983, p. 128.

38. Steve Frazier and S. Karene Witcher, "Debt-Swap Plan Is Proposed by Mexicans," *The Wall Street Journal,* March 15, 1985.

39. Alan Murray, "Feldstein Offers Assistance Plan for Debtor Nations," *The Wall Street Journal,* May 9, 1984.

40. Takeshi Watanabe, Jacques Lesourne, and Robert S. McNamara, *Facilitating Developments in a Changing Third World* (New York: The Trilateral Commission, 1983).

41. Statement of David C. Mulford, assistant secretary of the Treasury, International Affairs, before the Subcommittee on International Development Institutions and Finance, Committee on Banking, Finance and Urban Affairs, U.S. House of Representatives, March 20, 1986.

42. Under Secretary of the Treasury Beryl Sprinkel as quoted in Barbara Durr, "Sprinkel Refuses to Play Santa Claus for Bankers Seeking Federal Assistance on International Debts," *The American Banker,* December 10, 1984.

43. As quoted in Sandler, op cit., p. 77.

44. R.T. McNamar, "The International Debt Problem: Recent Progress and Future Ideas," Davos, Switzerland: Davos Symposium, January 30, 1984.

45. Sandler, op. cit., p. 76.

46. As quoted in ibid., p. 77.

47. Leland S. Prussia, "There's No Quick Fix for Debt Crisis," The Los Angeles *Times,* August 12, 1984.

48. Robert V. Roosa, remarks on foreign debt, Johns Hopkins School of Advanced International Studies, November 2, 1983.

49. *The Journal of Commerce,* "Scheming About the Debts," November 15, 1983.

50. Roger Lowenstein, "Cuba's Castro Finds Friends in Region by Urging West to Pay Off Latin Debts," *The Wall Street Journal,* May 23, 1985.

51. See Henry A. Kissinger, "Building a Bridge of Hope to Our Latin Neighbors," The Washington *Post,* June 25, 1985, p. A-15; and Riordan Roett, "Democracy and Debt in South America: A Continent's Dilemma," *Foreign Affairs: America and the World 1983,* Vol. 62, No. 3, 1984.

52. Kissinger, "Building a Bridge."

53. *The Wall Street Journal,* October 11, 1984, and February 4, 1985.

54. Gary Hector, "The Banks' Latest Game: Loan Swapping," *Fortune,* December 12, 1983, p. 112.

55. Ibid.

56. Ibid., p. 111.

57. R.T. McNamar, "The International Debt Problem: Working Out a Solution," Philadelphia, Pennsylvania: Fifth International Monetary and Trade Conference, December 5, 1983, p. 31.

58. Fritz Leutwiler, "International Indebtedness and World Trade," Philladelphia, Pennsylvania: Fifth International Monetary and Trade Conference, December 4, 1983, p. 4.

59. Jeremy Main, "The Argentinian Web Trapping U.S. Lenders," *Fortune,* August 20, 1984, p. 122.

60. *Federal Reserve Bank of New York,* Sixty-Ninth Annual Report, New York, December 31, 1983, p. 19.

61. Leutwiler, op. cit., p. 9.

62. McNamar, op. cit., p. 10.

63. *Business Week,* "A Hot New Market in Swapping High-Risk Debt," December 5, 1983, p. 144.

64. Albert Fishlow, "The Debt Crisis: Round Two Ahead?" in Richard E. Feinberg and Valeriana Kallab (eds.), *Adjustment Crisis in the Third World* (New Brunswick, New Jersey: Transaction Books 1984), p. 19.

65. Statement of David C. Mulford, assistant secretary of the Treasury, International Affairs, before the Subcommittee on Western Hemisphere Affairs Committee on Foreign Affairs, House of Representatives, Washington, D.C., July 31, 1984.

66. As quoted in Paul Blustein, "Volcker Criticizes Remarks on Debt by Fed's Martin," *The Wall Street Journal,* June 21, 1985.

67. McNamar, op. cit., p. 12. See also R.T. McNamar, "The International Debt Problem: Recent Progress and Future Ideas," Davos, Switzerland: Davos Symposium, January 30, 1984.

68. American Society, *Western Hemisphere Commission on Public Policy Implications of Foreign Debt* (New York: American Society, March 1984).

69. Leutwiler, op. cit., p. 9.

70. Ibid., p. 11.

71. Christine A. Bogdanowicz-Bindert, "Debt: Beyond the Quick Fix," *Third World Quarterly,* October 1983, p. 828.

72. As quoted in Alan Riding, "Clash of Views on Latin Plight," The New York *Times,* July 20, 1984.

73. As quoted in ibid.

74. Nicholas D. Kristof, "Debt Crisis Called All but Over," The New York *Times,* February 4, 1985; Gary Hector, "Third World Debt: The Bomb Is Defused," *Fortune,* February 18, 1985.

75. James L. Rowe, "IMF Cuts Off Lending to Mexico," The Washington *Post,* September 20, 1985.

76. Christine A. Bogdanowicz-Bindert, *Small Debtors, Big Problems: The Quiet Crisis* (Washington, D.C.: Overseas Development Council, April 1985).

77. Alan Stoga as quoted in S. Karene Witcher, "Debt Crisis Is Waning in Developing Nations, but It May Hit Again," *The Wall Street Journal,* March 26, 1985.

78. Peter Montagnon, "Top Bank Warns on Debt Crisis," *Financial Times,* September 23, 1985.

79. Albert Fishlow, "The State of Latin American Economics," in Inter-American Development Bank, *Economic and Social Progress in Latin America, External Debt: Crisis and Adjustment,* 1985 Report (Washington, D.C.: IADB, 1985).

80. Statement of the Honorable James A. Baker, III before the Joint Annual Meeting of the International Monetary Fund and the World Bank, South Korea, October 8, 1985; Art Pine, "Rea-

gan Aides Draft Latin Debt Initiatives," *The Wall Street Journal*, September 24, 1985, p. 32.

81. Art Pine, "Reagan Aides Draft Latin Debt Initiatives," *The Wall Street Journal*, September 24, 1985, p. 32.

82. John Burgess and Hobart Rowen, "U.S. Unveils Plan to Ease Crisis of Debtor Nations," The Washington *Post*, October 8, 1985.

83. Carol J. Loomis, "Why Baker's Debt Plan Won't Work," *Fortune*, December 23, 1985.

84. Ibid; Watkins, op. cit.

85. Richard J. Herring, as quoted in Peter T. Kilborn, "Oil Slump Delays 'Baker Plan,'", The New York *Times*, February 25, 1986.

86. Harold Lever and Christopher Huhne, *Debt and Danger* (Boston: The Atlantic Monthly Press, 1985).

87. Senator Bill Bradley, "A Proposal for Third World Debt Management," Zurich, Switzerland, June 29, 1986.

88. Stewart Fleming, "Baker's Tough Line on Third World Debtors," *Financial Times*, April 15, 1986.

89. Hobart Rowen, "IMF Sets $3 Billion for Low-Income Countries," The Washington *Post*, March 28, 1986.

90. Stewart Fleming, "De Larosiere Warns Banks of Need to Support Baker Plan," *Financial Times*, April 23, 1986.

91. David C. Mulford, assistant secretary for International Affairs, U.S. Treasury Department, "The U.S. Debt Initiative: Toward Stronger Growth in the Debtor Nations," before the Orion Royal Bank Conference, London, England: The Plaisterers Hall, February 4, 1986.

92. Art Pine, "'Baker Plan' for Easing Third World Debt Still Is Encountering Ho-Hum Reception," *The Wall Street Journal*, January 23, 1986.

93. Christine A. Bogdanowicz-Bindert, "World Debt: The United States Reconsiders," *Foreign Affairs*, Winter 1985/86.

94. James H. Gipson, "Two Theories for Outcome of Debt Crisis," The Washington *Post*, May 22, 1983.

95. International Recovery and Financial Stability Act, House of Representatives, Report No. 98-175, 98th Congress, 1st Session, May 16, 1983, p. 22.

SELECTED BIBLIOGRAPHY

Tamir Agmon. *Political Economy and Risk in World Financial Markets.* Lexington, Mass.: Lexington Books, 1985.

American Society. *Western Hemisphere Commission on Public Policy Implication of Foreign Debt.* New York: American Society, March 1984.

Bank for International Settlements. *The International Interbank Market.* Basle: BIS, 1983.

Barry C. Barnett, Sergio J. Galvis, and Ghislain Gouraige, Jr. "On Third World Debt." *Harvard International Law Journal* (Winter 1984).

Robert R. Bench. *A Framework and New Techniques for International Bank Supervision.* Washington, D.C.: Office of the Comptroller of the Currency, 1982.

Fred Bergsten, William R. Cline, and John Williamson. *Bank Lending to Developing Countries: The Policy Alternatives.* Washington, D.C.: Institute for International Economics, April 1985.

Henry S. Bienen and Mark Gersovitz. "Economic Stabilization, Conditionality, and Political Stability." *International Organization* (Autumn 1985).

Christine A. Bogdanowicz-Bindert. "Debt: Beyond the Quick Fix." *Third World Quarterly* (October 1983).

Christine A. Bogdanowicz-Bindert. *Small Debtors, Big Problems: The Quiet Crisis.* Washington, D.C.: Overseas Development Council, April 1985.

Christine A. Bogdanowicz-Bindert. "Small Debtors: The Smouldering Crisis and U.S. Interest in an Orderly Solution." Washington, D.C.: House Subcommittee on International Development Institutions and Finance, June 27, 1985.

Christine A. Bodganowicz-Bindert. "World Debt: The United States Reconsiders." *Foreign Affairs* (Winter 1985/86).

Edward Boyer. "Why Lenders Should Still be Scared." *Fortune* (December 12, 1983).

William E. Brock. "Trade and Debt: The Vital Linkage." *Foreign Affairs* (Summer 1984).

John Calverly. *Restoring Creditworthiness.* London: The Amex Bank Review Special Papers, January 1984.

William R. Cline. *International Debt.* Washington, D.C.: Institute for International Economics, 1984.

William R. Cline. *International Debt and the Stability of the World Economy.* Washington, D.C.: Institute for International Economics, 1983.

Benjamin J. Cohen. "International Debt and Linkage Strategies: Some Foreign-Policy Implications for the United States." *International Organization* (Autumn 1985).

Richard Coulson. "Banks at the Brink." *National Review* (February 18, 1983).

Richard Dale. *Bank Supervision Around the World.* New York: Group of Thirty, 1982.

Debt and the Developing Countries. Washington, D.C.: The World Bank, 1984.

Development and Debt Service: Dilemma of 1980s—Abridged 1985-86 World Debt Tables. Washington, D.C.: The World Bank, March 27, 1986.

Rimmer de Vries. "Perspective: Country Risk, A Banker's View." In Richard J. Herring, ed., *Managing International Risk*. Cambridge: Cambridge University Press, 1983.

Lamberto Dini. "Where the International Financial System Needs Strengthening." *The Banker* (September 1983).

T.H. Donaldson. *Lending in International Commercial Banking*. Surrey, England: Macmillan Press, 1979.

Economic Report of the President 1983. Washington, D.C.: USGPO, 1983.

Economic Report of the President 1984. Washington, D.C.: USGPO, 1984.

John Eisendrath. "How the IMF Makes the World Safe for Depression." *The Washington Monthly* (February 1983).

William N. Eskridge, Jr., ed. *A Dance Along the Precipice*. Lexington, Massachusetts: Lexington Books, 1985.

Euromoney. "The Country Risk League Table." October 1979.

Euromoney. "The IMF vs. The People." October 1983.

Federal Deposit Insurance Corporation, Office of the Comptroller of the Currency, and Board of Governors of the Federal Reserve System. *Interagency Statement on Examination Treatment of International Loans*. December 15, 1983.

Federal Reserve Bank of Governors, Federal Deposit Insurance Corporation, and Office of the Comptroller of the Currency. *Joint Memorandum: Program for Improved Supervision and Regulation of International Lending*. April 7, 1983.

Federal Reserve Bank of New York. "Sixty-Ninth Annual Report." New York. December 31, 1983.

Richard E. Feinberg and Valeriana Kallab, eds., *Uncertain Future: Commercial Banks and the Third World*. New Brunswick, New Jersey: Transaction Books, 1984.

Lynn D. Feintech. "Political Risk Assessment at Bank of America." In Theodore H. Moran, ed., *International Political Risk Assessment*. Washington, D.C.: Georgetown University, 1980.

Peter Field. "Meet the New Breed of Banker: The Political Risk Expert." *Euromoney* (July 1980).

Albert Fishlow. "The Debt Crisis: Round Two Ahead?" In Richard E. Feinberg and Valeriana Kallab, eds., *Adjustment Crisis in the Third World*. New Brunswick, New Jersey: Transaction Books, 1984.

Albert Fishlow. "The State of Latin American Economics." In Inter-American Development Bank, *Economic and Social Progress in Latin America, External Debt: Crisis and Adjustment*. 1985 Report. Washington, D.C.: IADB, 1985.

Foreign Broadcast Information Service. "Mexico: De La Madrid Speech on Economic Situation." February 22, 1986.

Andre Gunder Frank. "Can the Debt Bomb be Defused?" *World Policy Journal* (Summer 1984).

Lawrence G. Franko and Marilyn J. Seiber, eds. *Developing Country Debt*. New York: Pergamon Press, 1979.

Irving S. Friedman. *The Emerging Role of Private Banks in the Developing World*. New York: Citicorp, 1977.

Irving S. Friedman. *The World Debt Dilemma: Managing Country Risk*. Washington, D.C. and Philadelphia: Council for International Banking Studies and Robert Morris Associates, 1983.

Norman Gall. "Games Bankers Play." *Forbes* (December 5, 1983).

Lenny Glynn. "A Jacques de Larosiere Report Card." *Institutional Investor* (September 1983).

Jack Guttentag and Richard J. Herring. *The Current Crisis in International Lending.* Washington, D.C.: The Brookings Institution, 1985.

Jack Guttentag and Richard J. Herring. *The Lender-of-Last-Resort Function in an International Context.* Princeton: Princeton University, 1983.

Gary Hector. "The Banks' Latest Game: Loan Swapping." *Fortune* (December 12, 1983).

Jesus Silva-Herzog. "The Evolution and Prospects of the Latin American Debt Problem." Paper presented at conference "Beyond the Debt Crisis." London. January 27-28, 1986.

Robert D. Hormats. "The Outlook for the Developing Country Debt Problem." Washington, D.C.: The Joint Economic Committee, June 24, 1985.

Institutional Investor. "Country Credit Ratings." September 1983.

Institutional Investor. "Is the IMF Too Tough?" September 1983.

Institutional Investor. "Rating Country Risk." September 1979.

Institutional Investor. "The Credit Rating Shake-Up." September 1980.

Inter-American Development Bank. *Economic and Social Progress in Latin America, External Debt: Crisis and Adjustment.* 1985 Report. Washington, D.C.: IADB, 1985.

International Recovery and Financial Stability Act. House of Representatives, Report No. 98-175, 98th Congress, 1st Session. May 16, 1983.

G.G. Johnson with Richard K. Abrams. *Aspects of the International Banking Safety Net.* Washington, D.C.: International Monetary Fund, March 1983.

Anatole Kaletsky. *The Costs of Default.* New York: Priority Press, 1985.

Henry A. Kissinger. "Building a Bridge of Hope to Our Latin Neighbors." *The Washington Post.* June 25, 1985.

A. David Knox. "Resuming Growth in Latin America." *Finance and Development* (September 1985).

Louis Kraar. "The Multinationals Get Smarter About Political Risks." *Fortune* (March 24, 1980).

Joseph Kraft. *The Mexican Rescue.* New York: Group of Thirty, 1984.

Pedro-Pablo Kuczynski. "Latin American Debt." *Foreign Affairs* (Winter 1982/83).

Pedro-Pablo Kuczynski. "Latin American Debt: Act Two." *Foreign Affairs* (Fall 1983).

Fritz Leutwiler. "International Indebtedness and World Trade." Philadelphia: Fifth International Monetary and Trade Conference, December 4, 1983.

Ronald Leven and David L. Roberts. "Latin America's Prospects for Recovery." *Federal Reserve Bank of New York Quarterly Review.* Autumn 1983.

Carol J. Loomis. "Why Baker's Debt Plan Won't Work." *Fortune* (December 23, 1985).

Gordon Matthews. "Big Banks' Latin American Exposures Decline Noticeably But Remain Large." *The American Banker* (March 25, 1986).

Gordon Matthews. "Following Bank Holiday, Argentina Seems More Serious About Reform." *The American Banker* (June 17, 1985).

R.T. McNamar. "The International Debt Problem: Working Out a Solution." Philadelphia, Pennsylvania: Fifth International Monetary and Trade Conference, December 5, 1983.

M.S. Mendelsohn. *Commercial Banks and the Restructuring of Cross-Border Debt.* New York: Group of Thirty, 1983.

Edward L. Mercaldo. "Mexico: One Country's Attempt at Dealing with the International

Liquidity Crisis." *The World of Banking* (March-April 1984).

Ministerial Meeting of the Cartagena Consensus Debtors' Group. "Declaration of Montevideo." December 17, 1986.

Peter Montagnon. "Hopes Pinned on Baker Initiative." *Financial Times* (March 17, 1986).

Robert D. Muldoon. "Rethinking the Ground Rules for an Open World Economy." *Foreign Affairs* (Summer 1983).

David C. Mulford. Assistant Secretary of the Treasury for International Affairs. Before the Subcommittee on International Trade, Investment and Monetary Policy of the Committee on Banking, Finance, and Urban Affairs. U.S. House of Representatives. May 1, 1984.

David C. Mulford. Assistant Secretary of the Treasury for International Affairs. "The U.S. Debt Initiative: Toward Stronger Growth in the Debtor Nations." Before the Orion Royal Bank Conference. London: The Plaisteres Hall, February 4, 1986.

Pancras Nagy. *Country Risk*. London: Euromoney Publications, 1979.

Bahram Nowzad, Richard C. Williams, et. al. *External Indebtedness of Developing Countries*. Occasional paper no. 3. Washington. D.C.: IMF, May 1981.

Alexis Rieffel. "The Paris Club, 1978-1983." *Columbia Journal of Transnational Law*. Vol. 23, No. 1, 1984.

J.N. Robinson. "Is It Possible to Assess Country Risk?" *The Banker* (January 1981).

Riordan Roett. "Democracy and Debt in South America: A Continent's Dilemma." *Foreign Affairs: America and the World 1983*. Vol. 62, No. 3, 1984.

Felix G. Rohatyn. "How to Defuse the World's Financial Time Bomb." *Business Week* (December 16, 1985).

Graeme Rutledge and Geoffrey Bell. "Facing Reality on Sovereign Debt." *Euromoney* (November 1984).

Thibault de Saint Phalle, ed. *The International Financial Crisis: An Opportunity for Constructive Action*. Washington, D.C.: Center for Strategic and International Studies, 1983.

Anthony Sampson. *The Money Lenders*. New York: Viking Press, 1981.

Linda Sandler. "Is Discounting Sovereign Debt the Way Out?" *Institutional Investor* (July 1983).

Anthony Solomon. "Toward A More Resilient International Financial System." *Federal Reserve Bank of New York Quarterly Review* (Autumn 1983).

Statement of the Honorable James A. Baker, III. Before the Joint Annual Meeting of the International Monetary Fund and the World Bank. South Korea. October 8, 1985.

Harry Taylor and David Pflug. "The Overall Role of the International Banker and Key Considerations in Lending." In William H. Baughn and Donald R. Mandich, eds., *The International Handbook*. Homewood, Illinois: Dow-Jones-Irwin, 1983.

Time. "The Debt-Bomb Threat." January 10, 1983.

Eleanor Johnson Tracy. "Living With the Live-In Bank Examiner." *Fortune* (March 3, 1986).

Edgar Turlington. *Mexico and Her Foreign Creditors*. New York: Columbia University Press, 1930.

Henry C. Wallich. *Insurance of Bank Lending to Developing Countries*. New York: Group of Thirty, 1984.

Takeshi Watanabe, Jacques Lesourne, and Robert S. McNamara. *Facilitating Development in a Changing Third World*. New York: The Trilateral Commission, 1983.

Alfred J. Watkins. *Till Debt Do Us Part.* Washington, D.C.: Roosevelt Center for American Policy Studies, 1986.

Paul M. Watson. *Debt and the Developing Countries: New Problems and New Actors.* Washington, D.C.: Overseas Development Council, 1978.

Robert E. Weintraub. *International Lending by U.S. Banks: Practices, Problems, and Policies.* Fairfax: George Mason University, 1983.

The World Bank Annual Report. Washington, D.C.: The World Bank, 1983.

The World Bank Annual Report 1984. Washington, D.C.: The World Bank, 1984.

World Economic Outlook. Washington, D.C.: International Monetary Fund, April 1985.

Index

About the Authors

Ellen S. Goldberg is Assistant Director of Corporate Planning at Federal National Mortgage Association. She was a Senior Associate with Management Analysis Center, an international management consulting firm, where she specialized in advising financial services firms. She previously worked at the Office of the Comptroller of the Currency, American Security Bank, and Citibank. She received her B.A. from the University of Pennsylvania, M.B.A. from Columbia University School of Business, and J.D. from George Washington University.

Dan Haendel is an attorney with the U.S. Department of the Treasury, where he specializes in international financial law. He previously served with the Department of State, Department of the Army, and Citibank. He has taught at the University of Pennsylvania, Georgetown University, and the American University, and is a Fellow at Georgetown University's National Center for Export-Import Studies. He received his Ph.D., J.D., M.B.A., and B.A. from the University of Pennsylvania and his M.L.T. from Georgetown University.

DATE DUE